A Study in Econometrics: The Demand for Electricity in the United States

CONTRIBUTIONS TO ECONOMIC ANALYSIS XXVII

Edited by

R. STROTZ

J. TINBERGEN

P. J. VERDOORN

H. J. WITTEVEEN

1962

NORTH-HOLLAND PUBLISHING COMPANY – AMSTERDAM

A STUDY IN ECONOMETRICS:
THE DEMAND FOR ELECTRICITY
IN THE UNITED STATES

by

FRANKLIN M. FISHER

Assistant Professor of Economics, Massachusetts Institute of Technology, Cambridge, Mass.

in association with

CARL KAYSEN

Professor of Economics, Harvard University, Cambridge, Mass.

1962

NORTH-HOLLAND PUBLISHING COMPANY - AMSTERDAM

No part of this book may be reproduced in any form by print, microfilm or any other means without written permission from the publisher

PRINTED IN THE NETHERLANDS

INTRODUCTION TO THE SERIES

This series consists of a number of hitherto unpublished studies, which are introduced by the editors in the belief that they represent fresh contributions to economic science.

The term *economic analysis* as used in the title of the series has been adopted because it covers both the activities of the theoretical economist and the research worker.

Although the analytical methods used by the various contributors are not the same, they are nevertheless conditioned by the common origin of their studies, namely theoretical problems encountered in practical research. Since for this reason, business cycle research and national accounting, research work on behalf of economic policy, and problems of planning are the main sources of the subjects dealt with, they necessarily determine the manner of approach adopted by the authors. Their methods tend to be "practical" in the sense of not being too far remote from application to actual economic conditions. In addition they are quantitative rather than qualitative.

It is the hope of the editors that the publications of these studies will help to stimulate the exchange of scientific information and to reinforce international cooperation in the field of economics.

THE EDITORS

To Ellen

PREFACE

This study was originally made for the General Electric Corporation and completed in the fall of 1959. It was designed to show what modern econometric methods could contribute to the understanding of the forces shaping the demand for electricity. The Corporation had, of course, regularly made forecasts of the growth in demand, in connection with its analyses of markets. However, these forecasts were generally based on correlations of total electricity output with such aggregates as gross national product or industrial production, and threw no light on the mechanisms underlying the growth of demand and the circumstances under which past relations between electricity output and aggregate output might be expected to change. The Research Laboratory, to which I was a consultant, expressed an interest in the possibility that a more elaborate analytical technique might yield deeper insights into the probable future course of demand. I asked Professor Fisher to undertake the study, and offered him such assistance as I could. He is responsible for the whole of the econometric technique, which is a major part of any contribution of the study. I provided something in the way of collaboration in shaping the hypotheses that were tested, and in serving as an audience of more or less critical power on whom Professor Fisher tried out his models. In so asymmetrical a collaboration, I think it fair to say that I am equally responsible with him for the defects of the study, but that he deserves most of the credit for its merits.

We are both indebted to the General Electric Corporation for financial support, and for the patience, interest, and assistance in finding data of Drs. Kenneth Kingdon and Leslie Cook, the successive directors of the Project Analysis Section of the Research Laboratory during the course of the study.

Cambridge, Mass.   CARL KAYSEN
                                                            Harvard University

ACKNOWLEDGEMENTS

Any empirical study which involves as much data handling as did this one owes a major debt to the research and computation assistants who worked on it. Joan L. Bolker, Anne L. Kinnel, and Cynthia M. Travis provided invaluable help in acquiring data. Mrs. Travis, in particular, spent several months in the accumulation and processing of the data relating to consumers' stocks of selected major appliances discussed in Chapter 2 and tabulated in Appendix B.

The statistical computations here reported were performed by the Littauer Statistical Laboratory of Harvard. Among the many individuals, then members of the Laboratory's staff, who worked on the project—and space forbids my thanking each of them by name—were its director, Albert E. Beaton, Jr., C. Harvey Willson, and Beverly Scott. Miss Scott deserves a special note of thanks for the unfailing patience with which she performed the almost Sisyphean computations, the final versions of which are reported in Chapter 3.

The figures were drawn by Walter C. Eberhard and Ralph Hofmeister, and the manuscript typed by Grace C. Locke and Beatrice A. Rogers. Miss Rogers also assisted in the preparation of the index.

Zvi Griliches read an earlier version of the manuscript and gave us the benefit of his comments. If we have failed to profit from his advice in all instances, he is not responsible.

Finally, my wife, Ellen, read and helped edit the manuscript. She also patiently served as a one-woman sample for questions about the electricity consumption behavior of housewives and, as with most of my work, allowed me to continually harangue her with my ideas while they were being developed. It is to her that this volume is dedicated.

Cambridge, Mass.   FRANKLIN M. FISHER
December, 1960   Massachusetts Institute of Technology

TABLE OF CONTENTS

		Page
PREFACE		VII
ACKNOWLEDGEMENTS.		IX
INTRODUCTION AND SUMMARY		1
1. General Introduction		1
2. Households' Short-run Behavior		2
3. Long-run Household Demand		4
4. Industry—Constant Technology		6
5. Industry—Technological Change		7
6. Concluding Observations		8
CHAPTER ONE—ELECTRICITY DEMAND BY HOUSEHOLDS: THE SHORT RUN		10
1. The Model		10
2. The Estimating Procedures		22
3. The Data and the Results		28
4. Further Results: the Thirties		52
CHAPTER TWO—ESTIMATION OF CONSUMERS' STOCKS BY STATES OF SELECTED MAJOR APPLIANCES, 1944–57		61
CHAPTER THREE—ELECTRICITY DEMAND BY HOUSEHOLDS: THE LONG RUN		73
1. The Model: Alternative Specifications		73
2. The Data and the Estimating Procedures		85
3. The Results		91
4. The Rate of Electrification		113
5. Household Electricity Demand: Conclusions		117
CHAPTER FOUR—ELECTRICITY DEMAND BY INDUSTRY		120
1. The Constant Technology Model: Aggregation Problems		120
2. Estimating Procedures and Data		125
3. The Results		134
4. Technological Change		142
APPENDIX A—AGGREGATION OF INDIVIDUAL DEMAND FUNCTIONS		153
APPENDIX B—CONSUMERS' STOCKS BY STATES OF SELECTED MAJOR APPLIANCES, 1944–57		154
BIBLIOGRAPHY		185
INDEX		187

TABLES

Table   *Page*

1.3.1 Household Short-run Regressions by States, 1946–57 30
1.3.2 Urbanization and Short-run Income Elasticity 37
1.3.3 Tests of Within-Group Homogeneity, I 39
1.3.4 Tests of Between-Group Homogeneity, I 41
1.3.5 Household Short-run Regressions by Groups of States, 1946–57, I 42
1.3.6 Tests of Within-Group Homogeneity, II 48
1.3.7 Tests of Between-Group Homogeneity, II 49
1.3.8 Household Short-run Regressions by Groups of States, 1946–57, II 50
1.4.1 Household Short-run Regressions by States, 1934–41 53

2.1.1 Final Adjustment Factors: Five White Goods 71

3.3.1 Household Long-run Regressions by Groups of States: Washing
Machines, 1946–49, 1951–57. 93
3.3.2 Household Long-run Regressions by Groups of States: Refrigerators, 1946–49, 1951–57 97
3.3.3 Household Long-run Regressions by Groups of States: Ironing
Machines, 1946–49, 1951–57. 101
3.3.4 Household Long-run Regressions by Groups of States: Electric
Ranges, 1946–49, 1951–57 104
3.4.1 Household Long-run Regressions: The Rate of Electrification in
Southern States, 1946–57 115

4.3.1 Industry Regressions: Two-Digit Industries, 1956 135
4.3.2 Industry Regressions: Extractive Industries, 1954 141
4.4.1 Unadjusted Changes in Electricity Input Coefficients and Importance of Electric Power Costs: Two-Digit Industries, 1947–56 146
4.4.2 Adjusted Changes in Electricity Input Coefficients and Importance of Electric Power Costs: Two-Digit Industries, 1947–56 148

B.1 Consumers' Stocks by States: Electric Dryers, 1946–57 154
B.2 Consumers' Stocks by States: Freezers, 1946–57 158
B.3 Consumers' Stocks by States: Ironing Machines, 1944–57 162
B.4 Consumers' Stocks by States: Electric Ranges, 1944–57. 166
B.5 Consumers' Stocks by States: Electric Refrigerators, 1944–57 . . 170
B.6 Consumers' Stocks by States: Washing Machines, 1944–57 . . . 174
B.7 Consumers' Stocks by States: Electric Water Heaters, 1945–57 . 178

FIGURES

Figure   *Page*

1.3.1 Short-run Price and Income Elasticities by States, 1946–57 . . . 34
1.3.2 Grouping of States for Covariance Analysis 36
1.4.1 Short-run Price and Income Elasticities by States, 1934–41 . . . 58

INTRODUCTION AND SUMMARY

1. General Introduction

This study explores the application of various econometric techniques to the understanding of the factors determining the demand for electric power. Aside from the interest which such a study possesses because of its subject matter—for example, for the forecasting of power requirements—the work reported in the present volume seems of interest for the techniques employed. In particular, we deal to a large extent with a moving geographical cross-section of data and the analysis thereof presents an example of the results that can be obtained when standard statistical techniques are accompanied by theoretical and intuitive reasoning. The results rest not so much on standard tests of significance (although significance is frequently present) as on the plausibility of the pattern observed when the same—partly non-standard—techniques are applied to different sets of data.

The study of the demand for electricity falls naturally into four parts: demand by households, demand by industry, and short- and long-run determinants for each. In both households and industry, the use of electricity is complementary to the use of a stock of electricity-using equipment of some sort. In both cases, therefore, the short-run demand study is an examination of the factors that influence the level of use of a given stock of equipment, and the long-run demand study is a study of the factors that influence the rate of growth of that stock of equipment. In the household case, the rate of growth of the stock of appliances (including the number of wired households) seems to be more influenced by economic factors than is the case in industry, where the electricity input coefficients seem highly subject to autonomous technological forces.

The basic techniques which the study applies are multiple regression and covariance analysis. It is not our aim simply to get high correlation. It is always possible to get high correlation by using time series for national aggregates such as national income, consumer in-

1

come, industrial production, and aggregate electricity output. Such correlations generally have little analytical value; they simply reflect the fact that everything has been going up, but they are incapable of indicating possible changes in the rates at which one set of variables will move relative to another. Rather, this study attempts a detailed analysis of the interrelations of a large number of factors to see to what extent the results of statistical analysis are meaningful in economic terms. One of the more striking results of this endeavor is to show clearly that there are substantial differences in behavior in different regions of the country which must be taken into account in any explanation of demand. Thus, our technique generally requires detailed data by states for a large number of variables. Such data are not readily available; the major limitations of the study arise from the quality of the data, and a great deal of time and effort were required to construct some of the series used. The results of this construction are themselves of interest for future work.

2. Households' Short-run Behavior

The problem here is that of measuring the forces that affect the variation in the rate of use of the stock of domestic appliances (treating a collection of lighting fixtures as appliances too). Appliances differ both in the extent to which they are used (constant users of electricity, nearly independent of the behavior of the household, *e.g.*, freezers, as against variable users, *e.g.*, ranges or washing machines) as well as in their electricity input coefficients per hour of average use. Thus differences in the composition of the appliance stock among different communities lead to differences in responses even though the underlying behavior functions in each community are the same for each appliance.

The technique of analysis is to take a regression (in first differences of logarithms) of electricity consumption on real price and real income per capita for each state for the years 1946 to 1957. If the stock of appliances is conceived as an aggregate, measured in units of kilowatt hours of electricity use per hour of average use of appliance, then the regression technique employed eliminates exponential growth in the stock and provides an estimate of the average rate of that growth over the time period. Variations around smooth exponential growth are added onto the residual statistical error which the equations do not explain. The procedure also is designed to avoid the problems of serial correlation and multicollinearity.

The results show low (but frequently significant) correlations for individual states. When the states are grouped into areas, the correlations are much too high to be due to chance, and the groupings seem to have an important analytical significance. Covariance analysis shows different groups to be significantly different. Finally, the estimates of the growth rates in the stock of appliances which the regressions yield for the states are reasonable.

The states fall into two major groups, the first of which shows a near zero price elasticity and the second of which shows a much higher price elasticity, although still less than one. The first group includes roughly the states east of the Rockies, north of the Mason-Dixon line, plus the "Border States," and Florida and California. The second group consists of the rest of the nation. This grouping is topologically reasonable and it corresponds to a basic economic difference: the states in the second group are in a broad sense economically "younger" than those in the first group. The implication (which is supported by analysis of prewar data) is thus that as the economies of all states mature, short-run household electricity demand will become even less price sensitive than it now is.

The first of the above groups, in turn, can be subdivided into three subgroups corresponding to the degree of urbanization; the more urban states have significantly higher income elasticity than the less urban states. These last results suggest the following hypotheses to explain the response of household electricity consumption to fluctuations in real per capita income and the real price of electricity in the short run. First, there are significant differences in the composition of white goods stocks as between rural and urban states. In the poorer rural states the tendency may be toward more consistent use of "necessary" appliances such as freezers, etc. The richer urban states have a more varied use of appliances of a "luxury" nature such as smaller cooking appliances and air conditioners. Moreover, the "necessary" appliances are, to a larger degree, constant-use appliances. Further, in urban states activities outside the home which compete with the use of electricity in the home, *e.g.*, restaurants, movies, laundries, etc., are widely available. In rural states they are less readily available. A rise in income, therefore, probably tends to mean more use of electricity both inside and outside the home in urban areas, and particularly more use outside the home in rural states. Finally, a short-run rise in income in rural states may tend to speed up migration to urban areas (and thus to reduce electricity consumption in rural states) by providing necessary capital for such migration. All this would explain the relatively low or negative income elasticity in the more rural states. This set of hypotheses could be tested by survey data.

If the hypotheses are correct, there is a significant implication for future change. As urbanization increases and saturation is approached for more appliances, the difference in short-run electricity demand characteristics between urban and rural states will decrease. All this means that short-run demand will become more sensitive to short-run income fluctuations than it is now or than it has been in the past.

3. Long-run Household Demand

It is necessary to construct time series for households' stocks of appliances by states from rather imperfect raw material. Useful figures, though not of uniformly high quality, are established for the years 1946–57 for refrigerators, washers, ironers, ranges, freezers, dryers, and water heaters.

The model used to explain appliance demand is something like that for the spread of an infectious disease, the ownership of the appliance representing the state of being infected. A separate set of regressions is run for each appliance and, as before, the data from 1946–57 for each state, again in logs, are used, the states being grouped (because of the large number of variables) on the basis of the short-run analysis. The following are the variables:

(a) Changes in population
(b) Changes in the number of wired households per capita
(c) Number of marriages
(d) Changes in long-run income
(e) Current income
(f) Price of appliance
(g) Prices of substitutes (where relevant)
(h) Price of electricity
(i) Kilowatt hours consumed per hour of average use
(j) Price of gas (where relevant)

In general, net changes in the stock of appliances seem mainly to depend on changes in long-run income or changes in population and in the number of wired households per capita. The price of electricity seems to have nearly no effect; the prices of appliances only relatively small ones. There are two striking exceptions to the first statement. For both ranges and water heaters (especially in the southwest areas where gas is cheap) the price of electricity may have a definite influence. In situations in which the use of the appliance is near saturation, such as refrigerators, the only variables that are important were the demographic ones; whereas in the South and Southwest, where the use of the appliance is not near saturation, the economic variables are important as well.

In summary, these long-run results indicate that the growth of the stock of appliances is insensitive to the price of electricity within the range of experienced prices. Whether much larger differences in the prices of appliances than those previously observed would make a difference in the rate of growth of the appliance stock is not clear from these data, nor are these regressions a really adequate explanation of appliance ownership as such. They do suffice to indicate the effect of electricity price, however, which is all that is at issue here.

4. Industry—Constant Technology

The analysis of electricity demand by industry presents somewhat different problems than those encountered in the study of the household sector. These arise from technological change.

With constant technology, electricity inputs can be considered in two parts: one, used for lighting, heating, etc., which varies with the amount of installed capacity, but not with the degree of utilization thereof; and the other, used for production itself, which varies with short-run output. If every firm produced only one product, and if we observed each firm's electricity use separately, we would find that, in the long run, electricity consumed was proportional to output. However, the fact that we can only observe aggregate indices of production means that this proportionality is modified—since all products do not have the same electricity input value. This modification is of major interest, since it may be caused by changes in the price of electricity. When the price of electricity (to all firms) rises, certain processes—the highly electricity-intensive ones—become relatively less profitable or, if the consequent cost increase is passed on to the consumer, the prices of certain goods—the electricity-intensive ones— rise relatively and the demand for these goods relatively decreases. In either case, the composition of any output index shifts away from highly electricity-intensive goods and processes toward those of lower electricity intensity. This means that, for a given level of the output index, electricity demand by industry will be a function of the real price of electricity. Again, if the outputs of all products of all firms were known, total electricity demand would be determined in principle; given any aggregate index of output, the price of electricity is also needed. Further, this relation is of considerable interest, since it is easier to predict the price of electricity than to predict the output of each product of each firm.

To measure these effects, data on a broad—but not too broad— group of firms are required. Unfortunately, data are only available by very broad industrial classifications (two-digit industries) for a very few years. However, for 1956, sufficient data are available for ten two-digit industries *by states*, so that a cross-section—but not a time series—is possible. This raises certain difficulties of interpretation, as the use of such data means that the effect of geographical differentials in power costs (among other factors influencing industrial location) will enter the results. We thus estimate *upper limits* to the price elasticity of industrial electricity demand.

The results are generally significant and correlations are quite high. The upper limit to price elasticity is somewhat greater than unity in six out of the ten industries (highest 2.6, for the chemicals industry), unity or less in two more and zero in the remaining two (fabricated metal products and transportation equipment). Similar results are obtained for the mineral industries. Altogether, there is reason to expect a fairly high degree of sensitivity to electricity price in industrial demand given the technology of 1956. The paucity of the data makes it fairly difficult to be certain, however, and the effects of technological change are certainly more important than is the price effect just discussed.

5. Industry—Technological Change

It is difficult to say anything meaningful about technological change, as very little is known about its mechanism. All the data permit us to do is to study historical technological change—broadly conceived—between 1947 and 1956.

We look at percentage changes in the electricity input coefficients for all twenty two-digit industries between the two dates mentioned. We see the following: three out of the twenty industries experienced a decline in the importance of electricity, seventeen an increase (with the chemicals industry which almost tripled its coefficient, leading in size of increase), making no allowance for the effects of the fall in the real price of electricity. There was some—but not a pronounced—tendency for industries with large power costs (relative to total costs) to experience a smaller percentage rise in electricity input coefficients than did those industries in which power costs were a relatively low fraction of total costs. This may mean that industries with large power costs (relative to total costs) tend to act to reduce them.

When the effects of falling real electricity price are allowed for by applying the results of the previous analysis to the ten industries for which these are available, the situation appears essentially the same, save in one respect. The same tendency exists for industries with large power costs (relative to total costs) to experience smaller increases (or greater declines) in their electricity input coefficients than do industries with small power costs (relative to total costs). Now, however, the magnitude of the increases is less (naturally)—the chemicals industry which still shows the largest gain has only a 35 per cent increase—and five out of the ten industries show an actual decline in electricity input coefficient compared to three out of twenty (including one out of *these* ten), previously. Since our estimate of the price effect is a maximum estimate, the truth probably lies in between. At least one out of these ten industries (three out of the whole twenty) experienced technological change reducing the importance of electricity; at most, five out of these ten did (but probably fewer than ten out of the twenty, since the selected ten industries are those in which electricity is of the greatest relative importance). Technological change probably acted neutrally or increased the importance of electricity—the quantity of electricity consumed per unit of output—in this period.

6. Concluding Observations

The phenomena summarized above suggest certain important inferences on the long-run growth of electricity demand. In the household sector, as saturation is approached for any appliance, the growth in its stock depends heavily on certain economic and demographic variables—income, assets, number of marriages, number of households. For none of these is the relation such that the rate of growth of the stock of any appliance can be expected to grow faster than national income or population. The unimportance, in general, of price of electricity and prices of appliances means that substitution effects which might sustain a more rapid growth are unimportant. In the industrial sector, there are indications—though rather weak ones, due to the limitations of the present analysis—that there is some impulse acting to push technical change into channels that reduce relative power inputs in those industries in which they are comparatively high. Both of these conclusions point in the same direction: namely, that the continued growth of aggregate demand for electricity at rates two or more times the rate of growth of GNP depends heavily on continuing innovation. In the household sphere, a continuing flow of new appliances is needed; in the industrial sphere, what is required is a flow of new electricity-using processes sufficiently cost-saving to move against the possible tendency of electricity input coefficients to increase more slowly the higher are relative electricity costs.

These conclusions are suggested by the study, but this study alone is not enough to sustain them. In both cases, further exploration by means of sample studies in much greater detail is necessary. Household sample studies are a relatively well-explored technique; industrial sample studies centering on the possibilities for technical change and its probable impact on the demand for electricity present a new field for the combination of economic and technological approaches.

CHAPTER 1

ELECTRICITY DEMAND BY HOUSEHOLDS:
THE SHORT RUN

1. The Model

The demand by households for electricity is a derived demand. In the short run, the community possesses a given stock of each of a variety of electricity-using appliances and fixtures, which, for simplicity, we shall call "white goods." (This differs from ordinary usage in that our "white goods" include not only major electrical appliances such as home laundries, refrigerators, electric ranges, and the like, but also fans, television sets, electric shavers, and even light-bulb fixtures—although this last is not generally thought of as an appliance in the usual sense. Further, we do not include in our definition non-electricity-using appliances such as gas ranges, water heaters, or refrigerators. In short, by "white good" we mean any electricity using device or fixture the cost of the electricity for which is paid by the household itself in paying for its regular metered use of electricity.) The demand for electricity for household use is derived from the demand by the community of households for the services of its various stocks of white goods.

Now, different white goods have different properties. In particular, white goods differ as regards the degree to which a particular household desires or is able to vary the intensity of their use in the short run in response to various stimuli. It is difficult to imagine circumstances in which, given the type of refrigerator owned by a family, for instance, the electricity used for running that refrigerator would vary very much from year to year. The only such circumstance would be one in which the family varied its vacation habits, so that the period of the year for which the refrigerator was not in use at all (while the family was absent for an extended time) varied. While a family is at home, however, using a refrigerator at all means using it all the time; and such variation in the rate of electricity use as might be supplied by opening the refrigerator door more or less often, or changing the temperature control dial setting seems of the *de minimis* variety.

The case is very different with such white goods as television sets, however. Our national habits have not yet reached the point where using a television set at all means using it continuously. Even when the family is not away on vacation, the use of the television set can and will be varied as the availability of other entertainment both in and out of the home varies, or even (one hopes) as the quality of television programs themselves changes.

Similar remarks hold even for such appliances as dishwashers. The quantity of electricity used here will vary perhaps less than that used for the television set, but certainly more than that used for the refrigerator or freezer, as the family eats in or out of the home and as more or fewer guests are invited to share their meals.

In short, let there be n distinct types of white good. Let the average stock of the ith white good possessed by the community in which we are interested[1] during the period t be denoted by W_{it}. Let D_t be the total metered use of electricity in kilowatt hours by all households in the community during time period t. Finally, let the total number of time periods in the historical interval be to investigated be T. Then:

$$(1.1.1) \qquad D_t = \sum_{i=1}^{n} K_{it} W_{it} \qquad (t = 1, \ldots, T)$$

where the K_{it} are parameters representing the intensity of use of the W_{it} during the tth time period. They have the dimensions: kilowatt hours per time period per unit of particular white good. Our discus-

---

[1] For convenience, the model presented is postulated in terms of the community as a whole. If functions of similar form are assumed to hold for each household within the community, the community model may be thought of as an approximation to the sum of those functions. This problem is considered (although by no means exhaustively) in Appendix A.

sion above indicates that the K_{tt} will in general *not* be the same for different white goods and that they may be dependent on outside economic stimuli.

From the theory of consumer behavior, we should reasonably expect the principal such stimuli to be the personal income of the community, the price of electricity to households in the community[2], and the price of all substitutes for the services of electric white goods or for electricity itself. However, since the stocks of various white goods owned by the community are assumed fixed in the short run, the price of gas, the principal substitute for electricity in appliance use, should have no influence here. Similarly, since the possession of given stocks of white goods typically represents a collection of rather large sunk costs, the influence of the prices of outside substitutes for white good services, such as the prices charged by laundry establishments, should be fairly small in the short run. We shall later take such variables more explicitly into account when we come to consider the determinants of the desired stock of electric white goods and the demand for electricity in the long run. For the present, however, we simply take account of them by expressing the price of electricity in real terms. In the short run, there is no *single* really important direct substitute for electricity.

Letting P_t and Y_t denote the average price of electricity per kilowatt hour to households and the per capita personal income[3] of the

---

[2] It might be objected that the average household's electricity bill is so small as to make price effects non-existent. However, at least one of the authors was accustomed, when younger, to the phrase, "Turn off the lights; it costs money!" Households may adopt a cost minimization pattern even when the costs to be minimized are relatively small. Moreover, the proliferation of electric kitchen appliances has been accompanied by an increase in cost-saving opportunities. (Consumer magazines, for example, frequently discuss the economical operation of electric ranges, freezers, dryers and other applicances in rating such goods.) In any case, the question of the existence and size of electricity price effects is surely an empirical one.

[3] The reasons for using per capita rather than total personal income will be discussed below.

community, respectively, and expressing both in real terms, we have:

(1.1.2) $$K_{it} = F^i(P_t, Y_t)$$
$$(i = 1, \ldots, n) \quad (t = 1, \ldots, T)$$

where, of course, the n functions F^i need not be the same or even be of the same form.

It is convenient and not too unreasonable, however, to assume that these functions (or reasonable approximations thereto) are all of the same special form, namely:

(1.1.3) $$K_{it} = A_i P_t^{\alpha_i} Y_t^{\beta_i}$$
$$(i = 1, \ldots, n) \quad (t = 1, \ldots, T)$$

where the A_i, α_i, and β_i are all constant parameters. The α_i and β_i, of course, are the elasticities of the intensity of use of the given stock of the ith white good with respect to electricity price and per capita income, respectively. Further discussion of the functions (1.1.3), however, is best postponed until they have been transformed into different appearing but equivalent forms.

To begin such transformation, let γ_i be the kilowatt hours consumed by one physical unit of the ith white good in one hour of normal use.[4] These parameters are assumed technologically given.[5] Letting $B_i = A_i/\gamma_i$, we rewrite (1.1.3) as:

(1.1.4) $$K_{it} = B_i P_t^{\alpha_i} Y_t^{\beta_i} \gamma_i$$
$$(i = 1, \ldots, n) \quad (t = 1, \ldots, T).$$

----

[4] This is not always numerically equal to the wattage rating of the white good, because normal use may not involve the full capacity of the good. This is clearly the case with multi-burner ranges, for instance. It is unnecessary for later purposes to be precise about the definition of "normal use."

[5] Of course, there is no difficulty in the fact that white goods with the same name (*e.g.*, "refrigerator") manufactured at two different dates may have different γ_i. We simply agree in such cases to call such different units different white goods. In any case, the convention adopted below for measuring white goods stocks makes this problem non-existent.

Whence (1.1.1) becomes:

$$(1.1.5) \qquad D_t = \sum_{i=1}^{n} B_i P_t^{\alpha_i} Y_t^{\beta_i} \gamma_i W_{it} \qquad (t = 1, \dots, T).$$

It now becomes convenient to eliminate the γ_i by adopting a convention of measurement as to the W_i. We agree to call one unit of the ith white good that amount of that white good which consumes one kilowatt hour in an hour of normal use. (Of course, the fact that a physical amount of that white good with precisely that consumption may not exist is irrelevant.) In other words, we measure all white goods in kilowatt-hours-per-hour-of-normal-use units, thus setting all the γ_i equal to unity and eliminating them from (1.1.4) and (1.1.5), obtaining:

$$(1.1.6) \qquad K_{it} = B_i P_t^{\alpha_i} Y_t^{\beta_i}$$
$$(i = 1, \dots, n) \quad (t = 1, \dots, T)$$

and

$$(1.1.7) \qquad D_t = \sum_{i=1}^{n} B_i P_t^{\alpha_i} Y_t^{\beta_i} W_{it} \qquad (t = 1, \dots, T).$$

Now, let $\bar{P}$ and $\bar{Y}$ be the arithmetic means of P_t and Y_t, respectively, over the T time periods being investigated. That is, let

$$(1.1.8) \qquad \bar{P} = (1/T) \sum_{t=1}^{T} P_t$$

$$(1.1.9) \qquad \bar{Y} = (1/T) \sum_{t=1}^{T} Y_t.$$

Further, let

$$(1.1.10) \qquad C_i = B_i \bar{P}^{\alpha_i} \bar{Y}^{\beta_i} \qquad (i = 1, \dots, n).$$

Then substitution in (1.1.6) and (1.1.7) gives, respectively:

$$(1.1.11) \qquad K_{it} = C_i (P_t/\bar{P})^{\alpha_i} (Y_t/\bar{Y})^{\beta_i}$$
$$(i = 1, \dots, n) \ (t = 1, \dots, T)$$

and

$$(1.1.12) \qquad D_t = \sum_{i=1}^{n} C_i (P_t/\bar{P})^{\alpha_i} (Y_t/\bar{Y})^{\beta_i} W_{it} \qquad (t = 1, \dots, T).$$

This latter transformation is also equivalent to a convention of measurement, namely, to agreeing to measure Y_t and P_t as multiples of their respective means. Note that this is really a measurement convention and not a substantive assumption. An alternate theory of behavior would give rise to a form identical with (1.1.12) with $\bar{P}$ and $\bar{Y}$ *moving* averages. In general, such theories would assert that such moving averages represent the expected long-run value of the variables at time t, and that consumers of electricity react in the short run to deviations therefrom.[6] While this is a possible hypothesis, we do not espouse it here, although we shall use it in the third chapter. (Indeed the problems of testing it with the available data might or might not be insurmountable.) The interpretation of this formulation would be different from that of the present one. The justification of the presence of $\bar{P}$ and $\bar{Y}$ in our short-run analysis is conventional only, not psychological.

It is now possible to discuss the demand function (1.1.12) and the associated equations (1.1.11). The parameters α_i and β_i have already been interpreted. Set $P_t = \bar{P}$ and $Y_t = \bar{Y}$. Then the C_i are seen to coincide with the K_{it}. Since the W_{it} are measured in kilowatt hours per hour of normal use, C_i can thus be interpreted as the number of normal use hours the community uses each unit of the ith type of white good during a time period when price and income are at their respective averages. C_i is hence roughly[7] equal to the average number of hours per time period that a unit of the ith type of white good is in normal use.[8]

What (1.1.11) says, then, is that the number of hours in which a unit of the ith type of white good is in normal use during the tth time

---

[6] Examples of this general type of theory may be found in E. J. WORKING, *The Demand for Meat*, Chicago: Institute of Meat Packing, 1954; M. FRIEDMAN, *A Theory of the Consumption Function*, Princeton: Princeton University Press (for National Bureau for Economic Research), 1957; and elsewhere in the literature of econometric analysis.

[7] The equality would be exact only if $\alpha_i = \beta_i = 1$ or if $P_t = \bar{P}$ and $Y_t = \bar{Y}$ held for all $t = 1, \ldots, T$. The statement given is probably not a bad approximation, however.

[8] Since rough outside estimates of these latter parameters are available, we should theoretically later have a rough check on our results. In practice, the data do not allow this. See below.

period is equal to some "average" value (in the sense just discussed) times a power function of the percentage which price and per capita income are of their respective averages. The reasons for using this particular form are as follows (not necessarily in the order of their importance): First, the form is convenient; as just seen, the parameters thereof have easy interpretations. Second, any trends in the W_{it} can be expected to be exponential, for the reasons discussed at length below. The approximation to (1.1.12) that we shall use permits easy treatment of such trends. Finally, the form is not unreasonable. We should not expect equal increases in income, for example, to result in equal increases in the hours per time period that a unit of a particular white good is used, regardless of what the absolute value of income is to begin with. Rather we should expect a given dollar increase in income to result in a bigger change in habits and hence in the hours a unit of white good is used when income is low than when income is high. The percentage formulation used is a way of approximating this.

As for prices, the argument is somewhat different. The price of electricity to the household is likely to be so small as to make changes therein almost unnoticed. It is a well-known principle in psychophysics[9] that the size threshold for noticeable changes in stimuli is a *percentage*, not an absolute value. Again, (1.1.11) and (1.1.12) can be regarded as approximating this.[10]

A word may be in order here concerning the use of *per capita* income rather than total community income in our equations. In the first place, it is clear from the discussion in Appendix A that when our aggregate demand function (1.1.12) is regarded as made up of in-

---

[9] The "Weber-Fechner hypothesis," or "Weber's Law." See E. G. BORING, "Gustav Theodor Fechner," reprinted in *The World of Mathematics* (J. R. NEWMAN, ed.), New York: Simon and Schuster, 1956, pp. 1159–61.

[10] Of course, (1.1.12) is a convenient form in the sense that approximating it by (1.1.13) below allows many advantages in estimation which are described in the next section. However, this is not (nor should it be) entirely an independent reason for adopting (1.1.12) since many of those advantages stem from the same reasons given in the text that lead us to regard (1.1.12) as plausible.

dividual demand functions of the same form, some sort of average income is required, and per capita income is used as a simple approximation. In the second place, consider the following oversimple examples.

Suppose a community in which each individual has equal income. In year t various households move into the community and move out again at the end of the year. Suppose that the new households are identical in income, number, tastes, and white good stocks to the households already in the community. Then, using per capita income in (1.1.12), we obtain the result that electricity use will double in year t, a result that is clearly in accord with intuition. However, using total income in (1.1.12), we find that total electricity demanded will go up a great deal more than this.

Second, suppose that, with all other conditions the same as before, the new households are unelectrified and have no white goods at all. Then, using per capita income in (1.1.12) gives the clearly correct result that electricity demand will be unchanged, whereas using total income would give the unacceptable result that electricity demand will rise.

Some comments about these examples seem in order, however. First, as mentioned, the discussion in Appendix A shows that *some* average income is required; however, the best linear average to use would be one that weighted incomes by individual white goods stocks.[11] This coincides with per capita income only in very special cases such as the examples just given where all incomes are equal. However, the data will not allow any more refined treatment, and, to the extent that the difference in the two types of averages is proportional over time to the size of either of them, it will vanish in the estimating procedure described below.[12]

---

[11] The weights are quite unambiguous, since the measurement convention adopted as to white goods allows us to add the various stocks of a given individual household together to obtain a stock of a composite good. The details are given in Appendix A.

[12] The difference can at least be expected always to have the same sign and not to be randomly distributed, since we should expect the respective sizes of incomes and white good stocks to be positively correlated.

Second, it does not matter whether we use per capita income or income per household (as was implicitly done in the preceding example). If average household size is constant, this factor will appear in both the numerator and denominator of the income fraction in (1.1.12) and will cancel out.

Finally, a necessary part of the examples given is the assumption of changing population. If population were always the same, it too would cancel out of the income fraction in (1.1.12). More strongly, if population always grew precisely exponentially, it would cancel out in the estimating procedure described below. Population for most states does in fact grow roughly exponentially over fairly short time periods, but since population figures are available, there seems no reason not to use them and thus to improve our results.[13]

Now, (1.1.12) is a remarkably inconvenient and perhaps, in a sense, uninteresting form to estimate. It is inconvenient because even were enough data available to estimate the large number of parameters, estimation thereof would be computationally extremely difficult if not impossible. It is uninteresting for a general analysis of the demand for electricity since we should like to know something about the elasticities of *total* residential electricity demand by the community, rather than something about the elasticities of community demand for electricity for the use of particular kinds of white goods (although we could, of course, infer the total elasticity from the individual one, given all sorts of unavailable data). We therefore approximate (1.1.12) by:

$$(1.1.13) \qquad D_t = C \, (P_t/\bar{P})^\alpha \, (Y_t/\bar{Y})^\beta \sum_{i=1}^{n} W_{it} \qquad (t = 1, \ldots, T)$$

where the summation is permissible because of the units in which we

---

[13] As a matter of fact, the short-run regressions described below were originally performed ignoring population—that is, assuming exact exponential growth thereto. The overall results were substantially the same as those actually reported, but significance levels were somewhat lower, and the pattern reported below, though present, was much less striking. As we shall see, changes in the speed of population movements may partly account for that pattern.

agreed to measure the W_{it}. C, α, and β are assumed to be constant parameters.

Now, in fact, if (1.1.12) holds exactly, we cannot assume in any reasonable circumstances both that these parameters are constant *and* that (1.1.13) and (1.1.12) are identical. However, (1.1.13) may be a good approximation anyway, especially as (1.1.12) is only an approximation and cannot be expected to hold exactly. Whatever the "true" form of the demand function is, (1.1.13) may be just as good an approximation thereto as is (1.1.12).

It is nevertheless of some interest to discuss the parameters of (1.1.13) in the case where (1.1.12) holds exactly. Equating the right-hand members of (1.1.13) and (1.1.12), we have:

$$(1.1.14) \quad C(P_t/\bar{P})^{\alpha}(Y_t/\bar{Y})^{\beta}\sum_{i=1}^{n}W_{it}=\sum_{i=1}^{n}C_i(P_t/\bar{P})^{\alpha_i}(Y_t/\bar{Y})^{\beta_i}W_{it}$$
$$(t=1,\ldots,T).$$

It is convenient to distinguish between C, α, and β and the constant approximations thereto that will be estimated by estimating (1.1.13) rather than (1.1.12). Let these latter be c, a, and b, respectively. Now solve (1.1.14) successively for C, $(P_t/\bar{P})^{\alpha}$, and $(Y_t/\bar{Y})^{\beta}$. We have:

$$(1.1.15) \quad C=\frac{\sum_{i=1}^{n}C_i(P_t/\bar{P})^{\alpha_i}(Y_t/\bar{Y})^{\beta_i}W_{it}}{\sum_{i=1}^{n}(P_t/\bar{P})^{\alpha}(Y/\bar{Y}_t)^{\beta}W_{it}} \quad (t=1,\ldots,T)$$

$$(1.1.16) \quad (P_t/\bar{P})^{\alpha}=\frac{\sum_{i=1}^{n}(P_t/\bar{P})^{\alpha_i}C_i(Y_t/\bar{Y})^{\beta_i}W_{it}}{\sum_{i=1}^{n}C(Y_t/\bar{Y})^{\beta}W_{it}} \quad (t=1,\ldots,T)$$

$$(1.1.17) \quad (Y_t/\bar{Y})^{\beta}=\frac{\sum_{i=1}^{n}(Y_t/\bar{Y})^{\beta_i}C_i(P_t/\bar{P})^{\alpha_i}W_{it}}{\sum_{i=1}^{n}C(P_t/\bar{P})^{\alpha}W_{it}} \quad (t=1,\ldots,T)$$

so that, roughly, C is a weighted average of the C_i, the weights depending on the W_{it}, Y_t, P_t, α_i, and β_i; α must move so as to make $(P_t/\bar{P})^\alpha$ a weighted average of the $(P_t/\bar{P})^{\alpha_i}$, the weights depending on the W_{it}, Y_t, C_i, and β_i; and β must move so as to make $(Y_t/\bar{Y})^\beta$ a weighted average of the $(Y_t/\bar{Y})^{\beta_i}$, the weights depending on the W_{it}, P_t, C_i, and α_i. To a linear approximation, α and β will thus be similar weighted averages of the α_i and β_i respectively (compare footnote 6 of Chapter 4, below). In general, c, a, and b will depend upon the same things as C, α, and β.

We can say more than this, however, and the situation is better than it looks. Suppose that all the C_i were the same. Then a value of C $(= c)$ equal to their common value would satisfy (1.1.15) and cancel out of (1.1.16) and (1.1.17) leaving the latter two equations independent of the C_i. Similarly, if all α_i were equal, then a value for α $(= a)$ equal to their common value would satisfy (1.1.16) and the terms in $(Y_t/\bar{Y})$ would all disappear from (1.1.15) and (1.1.17) leaving the latter two equations independent of such terms. Similar remarks apply to the β_i. In the limiting case in which all three sets of such equalities held, it is obvious that (1.1.14) would be an identity and (1.1.13) (with constant parameters) just a restatement of (1.1.12).

In fact, our discussion above shows that these parameters cannot in general be expected to be equal. However, the real force of that discussion applied to the "average" number of hours per time period a unit of a particular type of white good is used—to the C_i—rather than to the α_i and β_i. These too should be expected to differ, but we should expect them not to differ too widely. For example, we should expect the α_i to lie mostly between zero and minus one, and the β_i to lie mostly near zero, as demand for the services of white goods should be generally inelastic. To the extent that the variance of the α_i is in fact small, α will indeed be approximately constant and c and b will depend only negligibly on the α_i or the values of $(P_t/\bar{P})$. Similarly, to the extent that the variance of the β_i is small, β will indeed be approximately constant and the dependence of c and a on the β_i or the values of $(Y_t/\bar{Y})$ will be negligible.

Furthermore, another and independent point can be made. To the extent that the α_i and β_i are all near zero, the dependence of c, a, and b on $(P_t/\bar{P})$ and $(Y_t/\bar{Y})$ will be negligible, as the variance of $(P_t/\bar{P})^{\alpha_i}$ over time will be small for any i (and similarly for $(Y_t/\bar{Y})^{\beta_i}$). To the extent that P_t and Y_t never get terribly far from their respective averages, this will be especially so. It follows that the point made above—that the dependence of c, a, and b on the particular time shapes of these variables will be negligible—is reinforced. Hence the errors involved by such dependence in using constant parameters in (1.1.13) will be small.

In fact, roughly, c, the constant approximation to C, can be expected to be equal to C at the point where P_t and Y_t are at their respective averages. At that point, (1.1.15) becomes

$$(1.1.18) \qquad C = \frac{\sum\limits_{i=1}^{n} C_i W_{it}}{\sum\limits_{i=1}^{n} W_{it}}$$

so that the weights here depend only on the composition of the stock of white goods.[14] Indeed, the above argument goes to show that the principal influence on the weights in (1.1.15) will be that composition, and that this, together with the C_i, will be the principal influence on the weights in (1.1.16) and (1.1.17). *This is as it should be.* We should expect the price and income elasticities of total residential demand for electricity to be weighted averages of the corresponding elasticities of residential demand for electricity for particular white good usage. It is perfectly reasonable and acceptable to have the weights be essentially the kilowatt hours used for the various white good stocks in an "average" year. Any other result would be suspect.

It is thus true, however, that the success of (1.1.13) in the event depends upon a constant composition of the stock of white goods over time. For this reason (as well as for those that apply to (1.1.12)),

---

[14] The fact that, as mentioned above, rough independent estimates of the C_i are available, means that in theory we can use (1.1.18) to check our estimate of C (for the average composition of the stock of white goods). In practice, the data do not allow this. See below.

(1.1.13) must be regarded as a short-run function. It will not do well over long periods nor when applied to communities in which the composition of the white good stock is changing rapidly. This conclusion needs some modification, however. To the extent that trends in the composition of the white good stock tend to be exponential in character (and we shall argue below that this is the general case), the estimating procedure used below will eliminate them and allow us to use a constant α and β (but not a constant C) as a good approximation.

Finally, we have reached the following important conclusion. *Even if the "basic" parameters, C_i, α_i, and β_i, are the same for two communities, the estimates of the parameters, C, α, and β, will not be the same if the communities differ as regards the composition of their respective stocks of white goods.* In fact, we can qualitatively predict the way in which the estimates of α and β, at least, will differ. A community whose white good stock is weighted heavily toward standard items like lighting and refrigerators or toward items whose use cannot be much varied will have lower (absolute) estimated α and β than a community whose white good stock contains proportionally more items like television sets. In fact, the underlying parameters, C_i, α_i, and β_i, would have to be very different for the two communities in order to outweigh this tendency. This conclusion also allows qualitative prediction of the parameters, α, β, and C, over time. It appears to be borne out by the evidence of the results given below.

2. The Estimating Procedures

We now consider (1.1.13) as the fundamental equation to be estimated, forgetting its origin until further notice.

Taking logarithms of both sides of (1.1.13) and adding an error term, u_t, gives:

(1.2.1) $$D'_t = A' + \alpha P'_t + \beta Y'_t + W'_t + u_t$$

where the prime marks denote logarithms and

(1.2.2) $$A = C\bar{P}^{-\alpha}\,\bar{Y}^{-\beta}$$

and

(1.2.3) $$W_t = \sum_{i=1}^{n} W_{it}.$$

Given good estimates of all the W_{it}, the natural procedure would be to subtract W'_t from both sides of (1.2.1) and thus to estimate the regression of $(D'_t - W'_t)$ on P'_t and Y'_t. Even were such estimates available, this would probably best be done by first taking first differences of both sides. This is so for a number of reasons.

In the first place, it is well known that economic time series tend to be serially correlated. This property in the dependent variable tends to reduce the efficiency of regression estimates. In effect, serial correlation means that the number of degrees of freedom available is far less than the number of observations. First differencing may serve roughly to remove such serial correlation and hence to give an honest picture of the significance of the results.[15]

Second, real price of electricity and real income per capita are likely to be highly correlated. To the extent that first differencing reduces such correlation, we are spared the difficulties of multicollinearity.

Third, we should expect the size and composition of the stock of white goods to be influenced by real per capita income and possibly by the real price of electricity as well. Such influences are the subject of the third chapter. While we should expect the existing stock of white goods in year t to be influenced primarily by an average of past incomes and an average of past prices rather than by the current values of those variables, nevertheless, we should not expect the size and composition of W'_t to be independent of P'_t and especially Y'_t, as the current values of price and income will tend to be highly correlated with moving averages of their respective past values. Estimation by least squares of the regression of $(D'_t - W'_t)$ on P'_t and Y'_t will thus give inconsistent results as there is more than one equation connect-

---

[15] See D. COCHRANE AND G. H. ORCUTT, "Applications of Least Squares Regression to Relationships Containing Auto-Correlated Error Terms," *Journal of the American Statistical Association*, 44 (March, 1949), No. 245, pp. 32–61.

ing the dependent with the independent variables. However, first differences in Y_t and P_t will tend to be much less correlated with first differences in their past moving averages so that inconsistencies from this source will be negligible after first differencing.[16]

Fourth, a somewhat similar point. It is, of course, the case that the price of electricity to the household is not a single number but a whole schedule of prices. We shall be using the average price per kilowatt hour as the best variable available. However, that variable is not the same as the marginal price per kilowatt hour, nor is it unrelated to the number of kilowatt hours of electricity consumed in a given time period. To the extent that such a relationship exists, our estimates will again be biased thereby.[17] However, several answers to this are available.

The above would be most serious if our consumers were subject to a two-part tariff. This is not the case, most electric bills in the United States being multi-step.

Next, our communities will be the states. To the extent that not all consumers in the same state are subject to the same rate schedule, the importance of the point raised will be reduced.[18]

Further, that importance will be additionally reduced to the extent that individual consumers tend over time not to remain in the same step of their rate schedules and to the extent that different consumers are in different steps.

---

[16] See F. M. FISHER, "On the Cost of Approximate Specification in Simultaneous Equation Estimation," *Econometrica*, 29 (1961). This point is of course related to the first one made. There we were concerned in the usual manner with the serial correlation of the dependent variable; here, it turns out that we have to be concerned with the same property in the independent variables.

[17] *Cf.* H. S. HOUTHAKKER, "Some Calculations on Electricity Consumption in Great Britain," *Journal of the Royal Statistical Society*, Series A (General), cxiv (Part III, 1951), p. 360. The point is that, given the step of the rate schedule, the average sunk costs of the previous steps vary inversely with the amount of electricity consumed.

[18] Note that this implies that our results below must be viewed with somewhat greater caution in the case of a state served by only a few utility companies than in the case of other states.

Moreover, whatever the form of the relationship between electricity used and average price given by the rate schedules, it is certainly not exactly logarithmic. It is thus not at all clear just how serious the bias in our results will be. It is probably safe to say that the bias is less serious than would be the case if the rate schedules were exactly logarithmic; however, too much reliance should not be placed upon this point since it seems obvious that the residuals, u_t, must be restricted by the rate schedules to some extent.

Finally, and most importantly, the relationship under discussion is one between the *money* price of electricity and electricity consumption. We shall be using the *real* price of electricity in our analysis. Further, while it is true that this difference would be unimportant if we were making a cross-section study of electricity demand, in fact we are making a time series analysis. Over time, the rate schedule relationship between the *real* price of electricity and the amount of electricity used can be expected to be almost non-existent, whatever is the case for the relationship with money price. This is so because the rate schedules tend to remain fairly constant while the price index shifts through time. *By taking first differences we ensure that the correlation between our real price variable and money price will in fact be low and thus that the identification inconsistency introduced by the existence of multi-step billing will be negligible.*

Fifth, we are here studying short-run demand. It is plausible to regard the first-differenced regression as the fundamental short-run reaction, as it eliminates slow-moving factors that are roughly constant over successive years. In particular, to the extent that the demand function contains exponential trends, first differencing the logarithms removes these by placing them all in the constant term. This point may be especially important when we consider the problem of trends in the composition of W_t, of the stock of white goods. We saw above that the usefulness of our equation (1.1.13) as an approximation to (1.1.12) (the "true" demand function) depends on a stable composition of W_t. Such constancy cannot generally be expected, however; rather, we should expect the composition of W_t for a given state to be subject to trends. Fortunately, however, such trends are likely to be exponential in nature. The chief trend in the composition of the white good stock probably comes from the introduction and increasing use of new appliances. To the extent that such new appliances are subject to a "demonstration" effect where the number of them sold is proportional to the number already in use, the stock thereof will grow exponentially. Such growth (for given kilowatt hour consumption per hour of normal use) will not show up in W_t as an exact exponential trend, but such a trend will be a good approximation. As already remarked, first differencing removes such trends by placing them entirely in the constant term which is otherwise of no interest in the first-difference regression.

More generally, and perhaps most important of all, first differencing allows us to avoid resting our short-run results on the uncertain specification of our long-run model. However long-run influences work, provided that they move slowly or in roughly exponential trend from year to year, first differencing removes them by placing them in the constant term.[19]

Finally, it will be of interest to compare the results for different states, both qualitatively and by means of covariance analysis. Roughly speaking, first differencing can be expected to remove influences on electricity demand, the effects of which, while they differ over states, are constant over time. This will enable us more clearly to isolate such differences among our state regressions as are of importance for the discussion of electricity consumption as a process taking place in time.

However, a word of caution is in order. First differencing will do all we claim for it, but we must be prepared to pay the price. First-differenced regressions tend to have lower correlations and higher standard errors than ordinary regressions from time series data. This is the defect of the virtue of the first point made above concerning serial correlation and of the inclusion in the error term of unspecified deviations from long-run exponential trend. To an extent, it is the

---

[19] For an extended discussion of this and some of the other points here made, see Chapter 2 of F. M. FISHER, *A Priori Information and Time Series Analysis*, Amsterdam: North-Holland Publishing Co., 1962.

reward of honesty. Besides, in the present case, we should not expect high correlations in our short-run results. There can be no doubt that while the model of the last section probably represents fairly well the systematic part of decisions on electricity use in the short run, such decisions are not generally of enough importance to the household to be entirely systematic. The amount of randomness in the degree of use of the stock of appliances in the short run must be rather large. This will be especially so in the case of communities whose stock of white goods is heavily weighted towards those appliances whose use will be little affected by price or income changes. *Before proceeding, the reader should reflect on how much credence he would place in an analysis of short-run electricity demand which resulted in very high correlations.*[20] While some of our individual results below are significant, the true test thereof is the plausibility of the overall behavioral patterns we find to exist.

Now, this discussion has assumed so far that good data on white good stocks were available by states. Unfortunately, this is far indeed from being the case. As described at length in the next chapter, we have with considerable effort secured estimates by states of the stocks of seven major appliances for the postwar years. These estimates range in quality, in our opinion, from somewhat below the sublime to a bit above the ridiculous. Estimation of similar quantities for other white goods, however, is simply impossible on any reasonable standard of accuracy. It follows that to estimate W_t by states and years with any kind of reliability is simply out of the question. It is thus imperative for our purposes to find an estimation procedure for (1.2.1) which in some way eliminates the need for such estimates.

Fortunately, one such is easily available, although we must pay for it by making an additional assumption. If the stock of white goods in each state grew exponentially (or with random fluctuations around an exponential trend), then ignoring W_t as an explicit variable and taking the first-differenced regression of D'_t on P'_t and Y'_t would give unbiased estimates of α and β by placing the trend in the constant

---

[20] This is not just an apology. We are later going to question some excellent fits on this basis.

term. There is, however, good reason to think that such an assumption would not be too bad. In addition to the demonstration effect mentioned above, the stock of white goods tends to grow exponentially because of the exponential growth of population—more especially because of the exponential growth of the number of wired households. It follows that it is not unreasonable to adopt the procedure just indicated and thus to obtain estimates of α and β which, while dependent on the exponential growth assumption, are independent of our particular measurements of the stocks of white goods by states. Accordingly, we shall do this. Of course, had we reliable white good stocks estimates, we should expect the more straightforward procedure to yield better results—not necessarily in terms of the parameter point estimates, but in terms of correlation and significance as our actual procedure places random deviations from exponential trend in the white good stocks in the error terms of our regressions, thus increasing the overall noise level.

3. The Data and the Results

As mentioned in the introduction, the communities chosen as units of observation were primarily the states. This choice was made not for any analytic reason—indeed, states are hardly homogeneous units—but because the state is the smallest unit such that full information covering the entire United States is more or less available for all variables.

The time period covered is 1946–57, inclusive.

As our quantity of electricity variable, we take the kilowatt hour sales to residential or domestic consumers as reported in the Edison Electric Institute's annual *Statistical Bulletin*. These figures are based on Federal Power Commission data. They are given separately for all states[21] with the exception of North and South Carolina, the data for

---

[21] Alaska and Hawaii were not states during the period studied.

For the postwar period, at least, electricity for agricultural pumping and irrigation is included in the highly heterogeneous "rural" classification and thus is excluded from our household data. All other farm service not on distinct rural rates is in our data. See Edison Electric Institute, *Statistical Bulletin*, Year 1947, p. 29.

which are aggregated as are the data for Maryland and the District of Columbia. Accordingly, we perform the corresponding aggregations on the other variables in the present analysis where necessary.

For our money electricity price variable we take the quotient of the corresponding revenue figures given in the same source divided by our quantity figures. (The difficulties involved in this procedure have already been discussed.) As our real price variable, we take money price divided by the *national* consumer price index. (It is unfortunate that the national index must be used, but no good estimates of state indices existed at the time that this study was performed.)

Finally, money income per capita estimates are taken from the Commerce Department's estimates in *Personal Income by States Since 1929*[22] for the period 1946–53 and in the August, 1958 number of the *Survey of Current Business*[23] for 1954–1957. These figures are then divided by the national consumer price index to secure estimates of real income per capita.

The results of applying our estimating procedure to these data are given in Table 1.3.1. Here the figures in parentheses beneath the estimates of α and β are standard errors.

The columns headed "k" and "autonomous growth rate" need some explaining. The former gives the estimates of the constant term in the first-differenced logarithmic regression when all logarithms are to the natural base. *This is not the same as the constant term in (1.2.1) which is eliminated by our first-differencing procedure.* Instead, it is an estimate of the exponential trend in the demand for electricity not accounted for by our explicitly included variables. The "autonomous growth rate" column is the same figure in terms of percentage growth per year. The chief source of this growth is, of course, the growth of the stock of white goods (remember that population growth is included in this). It is therefore somewhat satisfying to note that all

---

[22] A supplement to the *Survey of Current Business* (by C. F. SCHWARTZ AND R. E. GRAHAM, Jr.), 1956, Table 2, p. 143.

[23] R. E. GRAHAM, Jr., "Regional Income Distribution in 1957," Table 2, p. 13. Rough tests show that the slight break in comparability between 1953 and 1954 is of no importance for our results.

TABLE 1.3.1   HOUSEHOLD SHORT-RUN REGRESSIONS BY STATES, 1946–57

State	α	β	k	Autonomous Growth Rate (per cent)	R^2
New England					
1. Maine	—.0937 (.1663)	—.1556 (.1873)	+.1144	11.6	.2012
2. New Hampshire	—.3660[a] (.1309)	+.2320 (.2317)	+.0841	8.8	.5239
3. Vermont	—.0618 (.1218)	—.3874 (.1754)	+.0913	9.6	.6169[a]
4. Massachusetts	—.3451[a] (.1340)	+.3865[aa] (.1083)	+.0655	6.8	.6268[a]
5. Rhode Island	—.3184[a] (.1013)	+.4475[aa] (.1016)	+.0772	8.0	.7298[aa]
6. Connecticut	—.1278 (.1126)	+.2152 (.1199)	+.1137	9.9	.3054
Middle Atlantic					
7. New York	—.2103 (.1159)	+.1491 (.1286)	+.1156	8.1	.3008
8. New Jersey	—.2204[a] (.0873)	+.2738[a] (.0918)	+.0910	9.5	.5363[a]
9. Pennsylvania	—.2619[a] (.1037)	+.0724 (.1060)	+.1145	9.4	.4657
East North Central					
10. Ohio	—.1056 (.0847)	+.1105 (.0824)	+.1022	10.8	.2566
11. Indiana	—.2346 (.2175)	+.0873 (.1879)	+.1125	11.9	.1306
12. Illinois	—.0331 (.0636)	—.0097 (.0882)	+.1011	10.6	.0413
13. Michigan	—.1376 (.0699)	+.0651 (.0666)	+.0987	10.4	.3358
14. Wisconsin	—.1918 (.1338)	—.0257 (.0818)	+.1020	10.7	.2115
West North Central					
15. Minnesota	—.2178 (.1422)	—.2306 (.2145)	+.1068	11.3	.3067
16. Iowa	—.5182[a] (.1889)	—.0969 (.0987)	+.0955	10.0	.5226

[a] Significant at five per cent level.
[aa] Significant at one per cent level.

TABLE 1.3.1 HOUSEHOLD SHORT-RUN REGRESSIONS BY STATES, 1946–57
(continued)

State	α	β	k	Autonomous Growth Rate (per cent)	R^2
17. Missouri	—.2029 (.1614)	+.0884 (.1877)	+.1012	10.6	.1716
18. North Dakota	—.0625 (.3429)	—.2961 (.2099)	+.1545	16.7	.2108
19. South Dakota	—.2349 (.3551)	—.0982 (.1799)	+.1492	16.1	.0599
20. Nebraska	—.2499 (.2412)	—.1704 (.1911)	+.1238	13.2	.2075
21. Kansas	+.1490 (.1563)	+.0454 (.1447)	+.1360	14.6	.1333
South Atlantic					
22. Delaware	—.0347 (.1579)	+.1815 (.1056)	+.1275	13.2	.3310
23. Maryland and District of Columbia	—.2839[aa] (.0806)	+.4434[aa] (.1130)	+.0888	9.3	.6712[a]
24. Virginia	—.4649[a] (.1431)	+.2499 (.1381)	+.1132	12.0	.5822[a]
25. West Virginia	—.1417 (.2402)	—.2104 (.2365)	+.1147	12.1	.1172
26. North and South Carolina	—.5975 (.3459)	+.2578 (.3024)	+.1273	13.6	.2746
27. Georgia	—.1937 (.2353)	—.0630 (.2526)	+.1291	13.8	.1309
28. Florida	—.0999 (.1568)	+.0127 (.1304)	+.1613	17.5	.0762
East South Central					
29. Kentucky	—.2244 (.2734)	+.0392 (.2812)	+.1249	13.3	.0779
30. Tennessee	—.5373 (.5003)	—.1143 (.5501)	+.1317	14.1	.3208
31. Alabama	—.3971 (.2871)	—.3308 (.2302)	+.1369	14.7	.3635

[a] Significant at five per cent level.
[aa] Significant at one per cent level.

TABLE 1.3.1.   HOUSEHOLD SHORT-RUN REGRESSIONS BY STATES, 1946–57

(continued)

State	α	β	k	Autonomous Growth Rate (per cent)	R^2
32. Mississippi	—.7244 (.3801)	—.1824 (.2494)	+.1235	13.1	.3169
West South Central					
33. Arkansas	—.4993 (.3185)	—.1275 (.2643)	+.1099	11.6	.3396
34. Louisiana	—.9412[aaa] (.0276)	+.7453[aa] (.2007)	+.0808	8.4	.9933[aaa]
35. Oklahoma	—.2303 (.1479)	+.0431 (.2121)	+.1265	13.5	.2329
36. Texas	—.4242 (.3024)	+.2787 (.3867)	+.1302	13.9	.3032
Mountain					
37. Montana	—.8287 (.4252)	—.1035 (.3040)	+.0954	10.0	.3224
38. Idaho	—.6189[aa] (.1700)	—.3532 (.2460)	+.0852	8.9	.7076[aa]
39. Wyoming	—.6019[a] (.1865)	—.2716 (.3956)	+.1204	13.8	.6237[a]
40. Colorado	+.0376 (.1471)	—.1937 (.2134)	+.1423	15.3	.0935
41. New Mexico	—.6218[a] (.2615)	+.5054 (.7243)	+.1316	14.1	.4482
42. Arizona	—.9993[aaa] (.0134)	+.3387 (.3957)	+.0957	10.0	.9985[aaa]
43. Utah	—.5787[aa] (.1580)	—.0468 (.1075)	+.0840	8.8	.6459[a]
44. Nevada	—.6688 (.4231)	+.8847 (.3189)	+.0951	10.0	.4102
Pacific					
45. Washington	—.3790 (.1967)	—.1730 (.3864)	+.0949	10.0	.6173[a]
46. Oregon	—.5693[a] (.2267)	+.0525 (.4818)	+.0987	10.4	.5026
47. California	—.4073 (.3908)	+.6007 (.4224)	+.1028	10.8	.2018

[a] Significant at five per cent level.
[aa] Significant at one per cent level.
[aa] Significant at better than one-tenth of one per cent level.

these estimated growth rates are plausible ones (although only slight reliance can be placed on this point since a strong autonomous growth rate would show up in almost any analysis). The growth rates range from 6.8 per cent in the case of Massachusetts to 17.5 per cent in the case of Florida. The general geographical pattern of growth is about what we should expect.

It will be observed that, while the significance of the results is not high, the number and significance level of significant coefficients is considerably greater than would be expected by chance if no such relation as the one under investigation existed. The significance of the results is greatly enhanced by the considerations about to be discussed as well as by the results (reported below) of pooling the observations from groups of states.

However, before proceeding to a discussion of these matters, we may observe the following pattern. We said above that our approximation (1.1.13) would work best in the case of low growth and worst in the case of a community with high growth in electricity demand, since in the latter case the composition of the stock of white goods could not be expected to remain constant. This expectation is borne out by our results. The number of observations is the same for each state, so that the size of R^2 for the various regressions is a good indication of the relative degree of explanation which has been achieved. The Spearman coefficient of rank correlation between the states ranked by size of R^2 and by size of k is —.680 which is significant at the one-tenth of one per cent level.[24] There is thus considerable support for our theoretical proposition that our approximation works best in cases of relatively low growth.

Now, while the significance level of the estimates is too great to be due to chance, it is nevertheless true that it is not greatly impressive. However, we argued above that it is unreasonable to expect results at this point to be impressive from the point of view of standard probability tests, both because we have built deviations from expo-

---

[24] A value of 1 indicates perfect agreement between the rankings, a value of —1 indicates perfect agreement between one ranking and the inverse of the other ranking.

nential trend in the growth of the stock of white goods (and similar errors) into our error terms and because we should expect the random component of short-run electricity demand to be relatively very large. What counts here is the general pattern of point estimates of α and β, and here the over-all pattern is indeed compelling.

Figure 1.3.1 plots the α estimates as ordinates against the β estimates as abcissas for all states. We observe the following features.

First, the general order of magnitude of the estimates is not un-

FIG. I.3.I SHORT-RUN PRICE AND INCOME
ELASTICITIES BY STATES, 1946-57

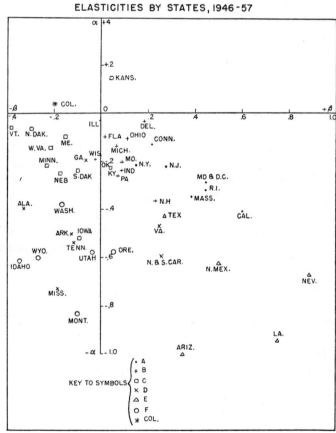

reasonable. (We shall discuss the plausibility of negative income elasticities in a moment.) No price or income elasticity is greater in absolute value than one, and practically all the price elasticities are negative. Further, the bulk of them are reasonably near zero.

Most important, however, is the way the points in Figure 1.3.1 representing observations for particular states fall. The sweep of the pattern is as follows. Consider the large bloc of states bounded by Canada on the north and by the Atlantic on the East, the southernmost members of which are Maryland, West Virginia, Kentucky, Missouri, and Oklahoma and the westernmost the Dakotas, Nebraska, and Kansas. Add to this bloc of twenty-six states Florida and California. The result is the group of states marked "Group A" – "Group C" in Figure 1.3.2. Note that the observations for these states in Figure 1.3.1 almost without exception fall higher than those for the remaining states. For the moment concentrate on these states only.

Looking at the points in Figure 1.3.1 that correspond to the states now in question, we see the following general pattern. Starting at the left, as we move to the right and slightly downward (*i.e.*, as we go in the direction of increasing income elasticity and slightly decreasing [algebraically] price elasticity), we tend to move from what may be described as rural states in the direction of greater and greater urbanization[25] until California and the states in the extremely urban East are reached. The only serious exception to this pattern is Illinois which lies with states like Ohio and Pennsylvania rather than with New York, Massachusetts, and California. As we should expect, Florida falls with the fairly urban North rather than with most of its southern neighbors. The pattern described seems to be one of three rough groups of observations.[26] The first, "Group A" in the two Figures consists generally of states with greater than 75 per cent urban

---

[25] Our use of urbanization here should not be taken wholly literally. Of course, for example, the pattern is also one of increasing incomes as we move from low to high estimated β values. We are using degree of urbanization as shorthand for a complex of variables all associated with the relative size of urban population rather than as the only causal variable involved. This should be remembered below.

[26] For this note, please turn over.

population; the second, "Group B," of states with less than 75 per
cent but more than 55 per cent urban population; and the third,
"Group C," of states with less than 55 per cent urban population,

FIG. I.3.2 GROUPING OF STATES FOR COVARIANCE ANALYSIS

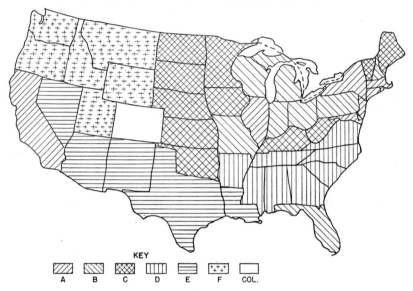

KEY

A   B   C   D   E   F   COL.

(Recall that we are restricting our attention here to the twenty-eight
states described above.) *Typically, greater urbanization seems to be
associated with greater income elasticity and slightly more negative price
elasticity with the first of these tendencies being very much the stronger.*
We shall discuss the reasons for this below.

Now to ensure that our remarks are not simply the results of an
optical illusion, consider Table 1.3.2. Here the twenty-eight states in
question are listed in decreasing order of percentage urban population according to the 1950 Census. The second column gives the actual percentages, while the third gives the rank of the state in the
list. Column four gives the rank of the state in order of increasing in-

---

[26] The choice of groups is arbitrary and the grouping is performed largely
to aid in obtaining summary results.

TABLE 1.3.2 Urbanization and Short-run Income Elasticity

State	Urban Population as Percentage of Total Population in 1950	Urbanization Rank	β-Rank
Group A			
New Jersey	86.6	1	5
New York	85.5	2	9
Massachusetts	84.4	3	4
Rhode Island	84.3	4	2
California	80.7	5	1
Illinois	77.6	6.5[a]	19
Connecticut	77.6	6.5[a]	7
Maryland and D.C.	76.9	8	3
Group B			
Michigan	70.7	9	14
Pennsylvania	70.5	10	13
Ohio	70.2	11	10
Florida	65.5	12	18
Delaware	62.6	13	8
Missouri	61.5	14	11
Indiana	59.9	15	12
Wisconsin	57.9	16	20
New Hampshire	57.5	17	6
Group C			
Minnesota	54.5	18	26
Kansas	52.1	19	17
Maine	51.7	20	23
Oklahoma	51.0	21	15
Iowa	47.7	22	21
Nebraska	46.9	23	24
Kentucky	36.8	24	16
Vermont	36.4	25	28
West Virginia	34.6	26	25
South Dakota	33.2	27	22
North Dakota	26.6	28	27

[a] Tie awarded average place.

come elasticity. The Spearman coefficient of rank order correlation between columns three and four is $+.7991$, which is significant well beyond the one-tenth of one per cent level. This indicates that the observed pattern is a strong one, for it tends to hold as among individual states, and is not simply a consequence of our arbitrary choice of groups of states as described above.

It will further bolster our analysis to test the hypothesis that our regressions fall into homogeneous groups and the hypothesis that the groups differ. This is done by means of the analysis of covariance. It should be remembered throughout the following discussion that the groups we choose are by no means uniquely defined. In particular, states like Wisconsin could have been assigned to Group C rather than to Group B and other dividing lines are arbitrary as well. (In fact, save for considerations of simplicity, there is no really compelling reason to have groups which are disjunct.) However, in general, we have avoided assigning states to groups *solely* because of their position in Figure 1.3.1; we always require some additional plausibility about the groups created. In the present case, the guiding principles have been geographic and demographic as just outlined.

The analysis of covariance as succinctly and very helpfully described in an unpublished paper by E. Kuh following Mood and Kendall[27] consists of three parts. In our terms, the first part is a test for over-all homogeneity of the regressions for the states in the group tested; the second is a test for homogeneity of α and β in those regressions (ignoring k); the third, which can be carried out only if the second test does not reject the homogeneity hypothesis, is for equality of k among the states.[28] This latter test is in two parts: the test

---

[27] E. Kuh, "Some Notes on Cross-Sections, Time Series and the Specification of Variables," paper presented before the Cleveland meetings of the Econometric Society, December, 1956.

[28] There is one conceptual difficulty in applying the analysis of covariance to the present problem. Like most statistical tests of hypotheses, the analysis of covariance is set up to minimize the probability of Type II error—of accepting the hypothesis being tested when it is false—for a given level of Type I error—rejecting the hypothesis when it is true. This procedure has the desirable property of biasing the test against the desired result; however, the analysis of covariance is designed for the case where that result is that the items being tested are *not* homogeneous, not for the case in which the hypothesis *directly under test* is the null hypothesis that the group is homogeneous. It would therefore be entirely unacceptable procedure to infer that if the tests show no significant lack of homogeneity at the 1 or even the 5 per cent level, the group in question is homogeneous. Obviously, we cannot misuse the

fails unless the first part shows linear state means; if this is shown, the latter part tests the intercept homogeneity hypothesis directly. We call the four variance ratios involved in the test F_1-F_4, respectively. Table 1.3.3 presents the results of these tests for: all states combined; that part of Group A consisting of small urban states— Massachusetts, Connecticut, Rhode Island, New Jersey, and Maryland and the District of Columbia; all of Group A; Group B; Group B plus the three large urban states of Group A—New York, Illinois, and California; Group C. An observed F greater (less) than the value in the same row of the last column means that the probability of obtaining so large an observed value is less (greater) than the corresponding probability given, on the null hypothesis.

TABLE 1.3.3   TESTS OF WITHIN-GROUP HOMOGENEITY, I

Group	Variance Ratio	Degrees of Freedom		Approximate Significance Points on Null Hypothesis
All States	$F_1 =$ 6.2884	138,	376	$F_{.001} =$ 1.41
	$F_2 =$ 7.1866	92,	376	$F_{.001} =$ 1.40
Conclusion: Homogeneity hypothesis emphatically rejected.				
Small Urban of Group A	$F_1 =$ 1.4768	12,	40	$F_{.10} =$ 1.71
	$F_2 =$ 0.6600	8,	40	$F_{.50} =$ 1.00
	$F_3 =$ 5.9612	2,	40	$F_{.01} =$ 5.18
Conclusion: Homogeneity hypothesis accepted as to α and β; specific test fails as to k but overall test indicates homogeneity.				
Group A	$F_1 =$ 1.6300	21,	64	$F_{.05} =$ 1.73
	$F_2 =$ 0.7961	14,	64	$F_{.50} =$ 1.00
	$F_3 =$ 3.3531	5,	64	$F_{.01} =$ 3.09
Conclusion: Homogeneity hypothesis accepted as to α and β; rejected as to k on basis of overall test.				

tests by requiring no significant lack of homogeneity at the 95 per cent level, but in the absence of better tests, we must insist on a significance level for lack of homogeneity which is somewhat greater (less significant) than 5 per cent. Fortunately, our groups raise little difficulty of this type.

TABLE 1.3.3   TESTS OF WITHIN-GROUP HOMOGENEITY, I   *(continued)*

Group	Variance Ratio	Degrees of Freedom	*Approximate* Significance Points on Null Hypothesis
Group B	$F_1 =$ 4.1464	24, 72	$F_{.001} = 2.63$
	$F_2 =$ 0.5772	16, 72	$F_{.80} = 0.70$
	$F_3 =$ 14.9651	6, 72	$F_{.001} = 4.34$

Conclusion: Homogeneity hypothesis accepted as to α and β; rejected as to k on basis of overall test.

Group B plus	$F_1 =$ 3.2217	33, 96	$F_{.01} = 1.89$
Large Urban	$F_2 =$ 0.7257	22, 96	$F_{.50} = 1.00$
of Group A	$F_3 =$ 9.2798	9, 96	$F_{.001} = 3.77$

Conclusion: Homogeneity hypothesis accepted as to α and β; rejected as to k on basis of overall test.

Group C	$F_1 =$ 1.2867	30, 88	$F_{.10} = 1.47$
	$F_2 =$ 0.5012	20, 88	$F_{.90} = 0.52$
	$F_3 =$ 3.1425	8, 88	$F_{.01} = 2.74$

Conclusion: Homogeneity hypothesis accepted as to α and β; specific test fails as to k, but overall test indicates homogeneity.

Thus each of our groups is essentially homogeneous within itself. We must now test the hypothesis that the three groups are different from each other. The appropriate test here is slightly different. The tests just reported were essentially tests of whether or not there was a significant reduction in variance when we went from state to group regressions. Now, however, we wish to test the hypothesis that there is a significant reduction in variance when we go from an over-all regression obtained by pooling all the observations in two groups to two group regressions. To eliminate the possible effects of differences in k among the states (after all, it is α and β which are of primary interest), we perform this test by first measuring all variables from their individual state means, thus suppressing the intercepts entirely. The test is thus one for significantly different α and β and only one

F ratio is required. The results for Groups A–C are given in Table 1.3.4.

TABLE 1.3.4 TESTS OF BETWEEN-GROUP HOMOGENEITY, I

Groups	Variance Ratio	Degrees of Freedom	*Approximate* Significance Points on Null Hypothesis
A and B	6.0894	2, 166	$F_{.01} = 4.74$
A and C	12.8207	2, 186	$F_{.001} = 7.1$
B and C	4.6528	2, 196	$F_{.05} = 3.04$

We thus conclude that our division of observations into groups is indeed a significant one. This conclusion is further borne out by the significance of the regression results for each group as a whole. Before reporting these, however, a word of caution is necessary.

To the extent that our division into groups was conditional upon the results for individual states, no significance can be attached to the finding that group results are significant in a statistical sense. It is always possible to secure the latter result by grouping together states (more generally, cells) with similar regression coefficients. However, our grouping was not that arbitrary. While it is true that the hypothesis involved was suggested by the individual results, the principle on which the data were grouped was an independent one, the states being first separated on a geographic, then on a demographic basis. This being the case, it is not at all trivial to secure significant results for the groups.[29]

We report two regressions for each group save where growth rates are inhomogeneous. The first is obtained by simply pooling all observations in the group, the second by first measuring all first-differenced variables as deviations from their respective state means. The second regression is the best estimate of α and β for the group, although,

---

[29] For a discussion of related matters, see FISHER, *A Priori Information and Time Series Analysis*, Amsterdam: North-Holland Publishing Co., 1962, Chapter 1.

naturally, in view of the results of our homogeneity tests, there is not much difference between the two sets of estimates.

TABLE 1.3.5 HOUSEHOLD SHORT-RUN REGRESSIONS BY GROUPS OF STATES, 1946–57, I

Group	α	β	k	R^2	Degrees of Freedom
Small Urban of Group A	—.2365[aaa] (.0464)	+.3281[aaa] (.0495)	+.0843	.4749[aaa]	52
	—.2409[aaa] (.0434)	+.3328[aaa] (.0021)		.5373[aaa]	48
Group A	—.2092[aaa] (.0505)	+.2875[aaa] (.0031)		.2695[aaa]	78
Group B	—.1873[aaa] (.0415)	+.0750[aaa] (.0014)		.1879[aaa]	82
Group B plus Large Urban of Group A	—.1679[aaa] (.0415)	+.0953[aaa] (.0016)		.0945[aa]	118
Group C	—.1623[a] (.0671)	—.1525[aa] (.0533)	+.1220	.1048[aa]	118
	—.1673[a] (.0624)	—.1443[aaa] (.0024)		.1266[aa]	108

[a] Significant at five per cent level.
[aa] Significant at one per cent level.
[aaa] Significant at one-tenth of one per cent level.

In these results, the low levels of R^2 are nevertheless highly significant in view of the number of observations involved. The parameter estimates are also quite significant. The pattern previously observed is now quite clear and significant. Moreover, the negative income elasticity in the rural states is seen to be very significantly different from zero.[30]

---

[30] A further test of the apparent relationship between urbanization and short-run income elasticity was attempted by trying to divide each state which included metropolitan areas of over one million population in 1950 into such metropolitan areas and the remainder of the state. (This was done

Now, how are we to explain this persistent pattern in our results? Why, in the group of states under discussion, does a greater degree of urbanization tend to be associated with more elastic (more with respect to income than with respect to price) demand curves? Further, how can we justify the persistent and significant appearance of negative income elasticities in the results for the rural states? The following hypothesis is offered as a *tentative* explanation. It seems to fit the facts before us, but part at least of the behavior hypothesized would be a fit subject for sociological investigation at the individual level. Such investigation is beyond the scope of this study.

We saw in the discussion in the first section of this chapter that two communities with the same underlying demand function (1.1.12) would still differ widely in their estimated demand functions (1.1.13) if they differed in regard to the composition of their respective stocks of white goods. A community whose electricity consumption came *relatively* from white goods like refrigerators and lighting fixtures would tend to have over-all average demand less price- and income-elastic than a community with relatively larger consumption from sources like television sets and electric frying pans. In fact, even if the underlying demand functions (1.1.12) were only approximately equal, this could be expected to happen. The relative positions of the points in Figure 1.3.1 corresponding to the states in Groups A-C may therefore be due in part to differences in the compositions of the stock of white

for electricity consumption and revenue data by securing data from the reports to the Federal Power Commission of those companies serving the metropolitan area and subtracting from state totals.) The analysis was then performed on each part. Unfortunately, we had to rest here on the heroic assumption that changes in income per capita in urban and rural areas within a state are proportional, since total state figures for per capita income had to be used. The results are thus not worth reporting in detail. A summary measure of the behavior of income elasticities, namely, the difference between the "urban" and "rural" income elasticities divided by the aggregate income elasticity for the state, averages $+17.5$ per cent for all the states involved and $+54.2$ per cent if California (which in Figure 1.3.1 could well fall with Group E below) is excluded. A positive sign is consistent with the pattern observed, but the variance is so large and the general character of the results involved so mixed that little reliance can be placed on this evidence.

goods among the states—especially differences between rural and urban states and communities.

In particular, the pattern in our results is probably due to a tendency for the stock of white goods in a rural community to be relatively more heavily weighted toward major appliances such as freezers, washing machines, and so forth than is the stock of white goods in an urban community. Freezers, washing machines, and the like tend to be greater conveniences if not necessities in rural than in urban areas. Where there is no nearby commercial laundry and cleaning establishment and where the substitute for a freezer is a series of reasonably lengthy and frequent trips to market, home laundries and home freezers are likely to be *relatively* more important in the white good stock than in areas where the outside substitute for such investment is literally right around the corner. Furthermore, rural states tend to be relatively poorer states. They therefore tend to be *relatively* lower in minor, quasi-luxury appliances than are richer, urban areas. Finally, rural states tend to use their appliances far more to capacity at all income levels than do urban states, as major appliances tend to be necessities. This reinforces the earlier suggested tendency.

With this in mind, the pattern of our results becomes quite understandable (remember that nowhere here do we find demand to be price- or income-elastic, we merely find relatively greater elasticity in urban states):

When incomes rise in the short run in an urban community, the level of household activities increases in all areas. Because the urban household tends to own a variety of electric appliances, the increased activity tends to manifest itself to some extent in an increased use of electricity. In a community already fairly well off, a short-run increase in income is unlikely to change drastically habits of living, but it is likely to intensify them somewhat. To the extent that urban households have followed the slogan to "Live Better" or at least to live more "Electrically," a variety of the things they do tend to require electricity. Of course, there is one tendency in the opposite direction when income rises. If higher income means less television and more movies; more generally, if higher income means more time spent outside the home, especially more and longer vacations, then electricity consumption will tend to go down with short-run increases in income. However, in an urban household, the easy availability of outside substitutes for home activities will already have made itself felt at low incomes. Short-run income increases are unlikely to induce enough additional consumption of such substitutes to outweigh the positive effect on electricity demand of more electricity using activity. More guests to dinner more often, more clothes to wash, dry, and iron more often, greater leisure to watch television or listen to an expanded record collection, and so forth, all mean a somewhat expanded use of electricity in the urban home when incomes rise.

The case may be somewhat different in the rural family, however. Here, we have already argued, the stock of white goods is weighted relatively more heavily than in the urban case toward the major appliances—in particular, toward items like refrigerators and freezers. Indeed, to the extent that stocks of minor appliances tend to be relatively smaller in rural states than in urban ones, the relative importance even of lighting fixtures tends to be greater. All these are items which do not vary much in their use when the family is at home. We should expect, therefore, that equal short-run percentage increases in income do not induce as great percentage increases in electricity demand in rural homes as in urban ones.

We can say more than this, however, and we offer the following hypothesis tentatively, as an appropriate subject for further sociological study. We argued in the case of the urban community that indulgence in activities outside the home which are substitutes for electricity-using activities within it tends to develop at reasonably low incomes (at least at the lowest incomes experienced since the war) because of the ready availability of such substitutes. Further, to the extent that urban communities (in the North) tend to be fairly well off, vacations are contemplated and indulged in before income rises take place. In rural areas, however, this is not the case. Electricity consumption within the home tends to be an inferior good, because activities within the home tend to be inferior goods. An increase in income will result in a definite change in habit patterns: in taking a vacation, in driving to town to eat or go to the movies, in going to visit relatives who live in another state, in short, in living more outside the home. However, all such activities mean *less* electricity consumption inside the home, not more, as incomes increase. [31]

Moreover, a stronger manifestation of the same type of behavior may be even more important in explaining our results. The postwar period was a period of migration from the farm. Short-run income increases may have affected the speed of that migration by providing the capital necessary to make the move. Clearly, however, the more rural the state, the greater the probability that households or individuals leaving the farm will also leave the state. Conversely, the more urban the state, the greater the probability that such migration will be net immigration into the state. However, population changes are white good stock changes; hence, to the extent that short-run income increases in rural areas helped to speed up emigration from the farm and short-run income decreases helped to slow it down, we should expect to find negative income elasticities in rural states (and the more negative the more rural the state). This tendency, combined with the factors already discussed, outweighs such tendency as there is to greater electricity consumption inside the home when short-run income rises—and we have already seen that the latter tendency is likely to be weaker in rural states than in urban ones. This helps to account for our results. [32]

Furthermore, we may make an additional comment. To the extent that, as we have argued, the rural community's white good stock tends to be weighted relatively toward appliances whose use varies

---

[31] Zvi Griliches has pointed out privately that this argument implies in part that the short-run demand for electricity in service industries should be more income-elastic in rural states than in urban ones. The data do not seem available to test this, however.

[32] The argument just given should not be confused with the similar *incorrect* argument as regards long-run, permanent income. High long-run income per capita in any state is likely to attract migration; we are concerned with the effects of short-run income changes on the *speed* of that migration— a very different matter.

negatively or not at all with income, we should expect the random component of the short-run demand function to be relatively more important than in the case of the urban community. Accordingly, we should expect to find somewhat higher R^2 and somewhat higher significance levels in the regressions for the urban states. More especially, this tendency should be especially marked in the small urban states which tend to have relatively more homogeneous populations. A glance at Table 1.3.1 reveals that this is indeed the case.

Now, if our results and explanation thereof are correct, the future should see behavior in Groups B and C, the fairly urban and rural states, approaching the behavior now discovered in the urban states of Group A. This is so, because urbanization can be expected to increase with continued and accelerated population growth, and, more importantly, because with rising incomes and continued sales promotion on the part of appliance manufacturers, the stock of white goods in rural areas can be expected to include an increasing proportion of minor, "high elasticity" appliances. Since the chief difference between Groups C and A seems to lie in the income elasticity of short-run demand, this tendency can be expected to produce considerably greater (although still not very large) sensitivity in residential electricity consumption to *short-run* fluctuations in income, at least in Groups B and C.

This concludes our discussion of the results for the twenty-eight states in Groups A-C. We turn now to an examination of the results for the states not included in those groups.

With the exception of the regression for Colorado, the remaining regressions all tend to share one property. While price elasticity is (absolutely) less than unity in all of them, it is (absolutely) somewhat higher than in Groups A-C. Further, these regressions seem to fall (although much more crudely than in the case of Groups A-C)into three groups. The first and largest of these, Group D, consists of the states of the old Confederacy east of the Mississippi River, excluding Florida, plus Arkansas. Texas may also belong to this group. The second group, Group E, consists of Louisiana, New Mexico, Arizona, Nevada, and possibly Texas. (Note that California falls close to this group.) Finally, the last group, Group F, consists of Wyoming, Montana, Idaho, Utah, Washington, and Oregon.[33]

As before, we test for homogeneity among the states within a group by covariance analysis. Table 1.3.6 presents these results.

TABLE 1.3.6   TESTS OF WITHIN-GROUP HOMOGENEITY, II

Group	Variance Ratio	Degrees of Freedom		Approximate Significance Points on Null Hypothesis
Group D	$F_1 = 0.5583$	18,	56	$F_{.80} = 0.71$
	$F_2 = 0.4911$	12,	56	$F_{.90} = 0.51$
	$F_3 = 0.5725$	4,	56	$F_{.05} = 2.53$
	$F_4 = 0.9331$	2,	56	$F_{.50} = 1.00$
Conclusion: Homogeneity hypothesis accepted on all counts.				
Group D plus	$F_1 = 0.5961$	21,	64	$F_{.90} = 0.60$
Texas	$F_2 = 0.5298$	14,	64	$F_{.90} = 0.55$
	$F_3 = 0.5817$	5,	64	$F_{.05} = 2.36$
	$F_4 = 1.0966$	2,	64	$F_{.20} = 1.65$
Conclusion: Homogeneity hypothesis accepted on all counts.				
Group E	$F_1 = 1.1087$	9,	32	$F_{.20} = 1.48$
	$F_2 = 1.3300$	6,	32	$F_{.20} = 1.53$
	$F_3 = 1.2524$	1,	32	$F_{.05} = 4.16$
	$F_4 = 0.3730$	2,	32	$F_{.90} = 0.40$
Conclusion: Homogeneity hypothesis accepted on all counts.				

(continued on next page)

---

[33] Our grouping of states now accounts for all states save Colorado. It is difficult to make any decision here. In its eastern portions, Colorado resembles the plains states, but it has a much higher urban population than these. One choice would be to place it in Group B, where its urban percentage would put it were it included with the first three groups. Despite its negative income elasticity, such a decision would not appreciably change the results or analysis reported above, especially in view of the very low multiple correlation obtained. On the other hand, such a choice seems implausible for *a priori* reasons. The western and urban part of the state resembles more the states of Group F than the states of the urban Midwest and East. However, the regression results are far away from the results for such states, although perhaps not terribly significantly so. It seems best to conclude that the state is an inhomogeneous one and to leave it out of all groups rather than try to force it into any preconceived mold.

TABLE 1.3.6   TESTS OF WITHIN-GROUP HOMOGENEITY, II   *(continued)*

Group	Variance Ratio	Degrees of Freedom		*Approximate* Significance Points on Null Hypothesis
Group E plus	$F_1 = 1.0553$	12,	40	$F_{.20} = 1.41$
Texas	$F_2 = 1.2807$	8,	40	$F_{.20} = 1.47$
	$F_3 = 0.7789$	2,	40	$F_{.05} = 3.23$
	$F_4 = 0.4304$	2,	40	$F_{.50} = 1.00$

Conclusion: Homogeneity hypothesis accepted on all counts.

Group F	$F_1 = 0.7209$	15,	48	$F_{.50} = 1.00$
	$F_2 = 0.2844$	10,	48	$F_{.95} = 0.35$
	$F_3 = 0.8068$	3,	48	$F_{.05} = 2.81$
	$F_4 = 2.7741$	2,	48	$F_{.05} = 3.27$

Conclusion: Homogeneity hypothesis accepted as to α and β; homogeneity hypothesis accepted as to k principally on evidence of overall test.

On the basis of the comparative results above we henceforward place Texas with Group E, the Southwest, rather than with Group D, the South.

Table 1.3.7 presents the results of tests for significant inhomogeneity between all pairs of group not previously reported. The same test as before was used.

TABLE 1.3.7   TESTS OF BETWEEN-GROUP HOMOGENEITY, II

Groups	Variance Ratio	Degrees of Freedom		*Approximate* Significance Points On Null Hypothesis
A and D	12.7882	2,	146	$F_{.001} = 7.2$
A and E	47.2299	2,	126	$F_{.001} = 7.3$
A and F	24.8316	2,	136	$F_{.001} = 7.3$
B and D	6.4265	2,	156	$F_{.01} = 4.8$
B and E	74.1708	2,	136	$F_{.001} = 7.3$
B and F	17.3613	2,	146	$F_{.001} = 7.2$
C and D	3.1003	2,	187	$F_{.05} = 3.04$
C and E	95.3039	2,	156	$F_{.001} = 7.2$
C and F	9.0065	2,	166	$F_{.001} = 7.1$
D and E	21.1534	2,	116	$F_{.001} = 7.3$
D and F	0.8007	2,	126	$F_{.50} = 1.00$
E and F	25.0295	2,	126	$F_{.001} = 7.2$

All of these pairs show highly significant inhomogeneities with the exception of C and D (significant on five per cent level) and D and F (not significant). There is certainly no doubt that Groups A-C are not drawn from the same populations as Groups D-F. On *a priori* grounds it seems unreasonable to lump the Southern and Mountain states together, so we continue to distinguish between Groups D and F.

Table 1.3.8 presents the Group regressions for Groups D-F. As before, two regressions are presented for each Group, the first with all observations simply pooled, and the second suppressing differences in individual state k.

TABLE 1.3.8   HOUSEHOLD SHORT-RUN REGRESSIONS BY GROUPS OF STATES, 1946–57, II

Group	α	β	k	R^2	Degrees of Freedom
Group D	—.4717aaa (.1024)	—.0592 (.0916)	+.1253	.2626aaa	74
	—.4515aaa (.1049)	—.0582aaa (.0086)		.2543aaa	68
Group E	—.9974aaa (.0102)	+.8901aaa (.1531)	+.0839	.9944aaa	52
	—.9957aaa (.0108)	+.8664aaa (.0255)		.9942aaa	48
Group F	—.6295aaa (.0821)	—.0778 (.0991)	+.0942	.5066aaa	63
	—.5975aaa (.0807)	—.0969aaa (.0093)		.5174aaa	58

aaa Significant at one-tenth of one per cent level.

Now, it would be possible to argue that to some extent the same mechanisms that we claimed operated in Groups A-C operate in Groups D-F also. There is some tendency for richer and relatively more urban states to have greater income and price elasticity than do poorer and relatively more rural areas. This tendency is by no means clear, however. What does show up strongly is the tendency to negative income elasticities in Groups D and F, as we should now expect for predominantly rural states.

However, all this is dwarfed beside the very strong tendency for states in these groups to have markedly (absolutely) greater price elasticity than do the states of the North and East—Groups A-C. Unlike the difference between urban and rural states in the latter groups, this difference in price elasticity does not seem to be susceptible to explanation solely, or even largely in terms of differences in the composition of the stock of white goods. If anything, we should expect the composition of the white good stock in the South to be weighted toward low-elasticity goods, and the effect observed is one of high elasticity. We conclude, therefore, that the difference lies deeper than this. It must be a difference in the underlying demand functions (1.1.12), rather than only in the approximations thereto (1.1.13). The high price elasticities in Groups D-F appear to stem from the structure of the demand relation and not simply from the weighting of our estimates.

Furthermore, this underlying difference is not easily explained. One partial explanation may be that the states under discussion are largely the lowest income states. At very low incomes, the electricity bill may bulk larger in the budget than it does at higher income levels, so that more attention is paid to the cost of electricity consumption.[34] Further, the habits of appliance use may be so newly formed that the labor of the housewife is an acceptable or even usual substitute for the services of some appliances when the cost of using the latter rises. Certainly, there seems to exist a tendency for economically younger states to have a more price-elastic demand.

It cannot be pretended, however, that these speculations provide a complete explanation, although they are considerably buttressed by the results of the next section. We must therefore, to some extent, be content with taking the tendency to higher (absolute) price elasticities in Groups D-F as an unexplained datum. This is not terribly disturbing, however. There is really no reason to expect the underlying demand functions investigated to be the same over all states, and the results for these groups are not at all implausible—they are

---

[34] The Weber-Fechner hypothesis again.

simply different. What is reassuring is that the states within which such different tendencies are found are plausibly lumped together. We should be greatly disturbed to find Maine or Ohio in this group, for example, but there is nothing disturbing in the pattern discovered. The underlying short-run demand for electricity in the economically younger states of the South and part of the Northwest simply displays somewhat different characteristics from the corresponding function in the economically older states of the North, Midwest, and East. The fact that Florida and California seem to lie with the latter states is doubly reassuring.

4. Further Results: the Thirties

It is of considerable interest to compare the results discussed above with those obtained when the same procedure is applied to prewar data. Data are not as readily accessible for these years as for the later period; we use unpublished data furnished by the Edison Electric Institute. These data are for the years 1934–41, inclusive, and are complete for all but four states, which we omit. They are not strictly comparable with the data for the postwar years, as they include more farm electricity demand than do the later data, owing to changes in classifications. The results are presented in Table 1.4.1. Note that the number of degrees of freedom here is four, rather than eight as in Table 1.3.1.

These results are striking indeed. In fact, they are so striking as to be a little suspect. Let us discuss this before going on to an examination of the implications of the results, if genuine.

We asked the reader, above, to consider how much credence he would place in an analysis of the intensity of appliance use that had no large random component. Of course, that request was made with the results of Table 1.3.1 in mind, but in asking it we wielded a two-edged sword. It is simply difficult to believe in results that almost consistently explain 99.9 per cent of the variance in short-run electricity demand. Of course, the fact that we have only four degrees of freedom here means that fairly high correlations are to be expected,

TABLE 1.4.1 HOUSEHOLD SHORT-RUN REGRESSIONS BY STATES, 1934–41

State	α	β	k	Autonomous Growth Rate (per cent)	R^2
New England					
1. Maine	—1.0083[aaa] (0.0065)	—0.1251 (0.0861)	+.0515	5.3	.9998[aaa]
2. New Hampshire	—0.9877[aaa] (0.0175)	—0.1568 (0.2675)	+.0541	5.6	.9996[aaa]
3. Vermont	—0.7015[a] (0.2309)	—0.0178 (0.1031)	+.0551	5.7	.6994
4. Massachusetts	—0.9952[aaa] (0.0075)	+0.0064 (0.1275)	+.0345	3.5	.9998[aaa]
5. Rhode Island	—0.9877[aaa] (0.0069)	+0.1673 (0.0917)	+.0157	1.6	.9998[aaa]
6. Connecticut	—1.0146[aaa] (0.0061)	+0.1004 (0.0837)	+.0407	4.2	.9998[aaa]
Middle Atlantic					
7. New York	—1.0028[aaa] (0.0031)	—0.0951 (0.0796)	+.0393	4.0	.9999[aaa]
8. New Jersey	—0.9991[aaa] (0.0039)	—0.0122 (0.1043)	+.0423	4.3	.9999[aaa]
9. Pennsylvania	—0.9910[aaa] (0.0053)	+0.0409 (0.0600)	+.0381	3.9	.9988[aaa]
East North Central					
10. Ohio	—1.0187[aaa] (0.0219)	—0.0463 (0.1162)	+.0528	5.4	.9983[aaa]
11. Indiana	—0.9995[aaa] (0.0064)	—0.0977 (0.1337)	+.0676	7.0	.9998[aaa]
12. Illinois	—1.0043[aaa] (0.0056)	—0.1396 (0.0598)	+.0512	5.2	.9999[aaa]
13. Michigan	—1.0087[aaa] (0.0076)	—0.0362 (0.0792)	+.0839	8.7	.9997[aaa]
14. Wisconsin	—0.9955[aaa] (0.0226)	—0.0689 (0.3293)	+.0401	4.1	.9982[aaa]
West North Central					
15. Minnesota	—0.9928[aaa] (0.0247)	—0.1445 (0.2873)	+.0527	5.4	.9985[aaa]

[a] Significant at five per cent level.
[aaa] Significant at one-tenth of one per cent level.

TABLE 1.4.1 HOUSEHOLD SHORT-RUN REGRESSIONS BY STATES, 1934–41
(continued)

State	α	β	k	Autonomous Growth Rate (per cent)	R^2
16. Iowa	Data are incomplete.				
17. Missouri	—0.9901[aaa] (0.0141)	+0.2028 (0.2462)	+.0281	2.8	.9994[aaa]
18. North Dakota	—0.6322 (0.3280)	+0.0274 (0.0835)	+.0768	8.0	.4952
19. South Dakota	—0.2591 (0.3779)	—0.0269 (0.0800)	+.0787	8.2	.1083
20. Nebraska	—0.9978[aaa] (0.0375)	+0.0237 (0.1900)	+.0239	2.4	.9946[aaa]
21. Kansas	Data are incomplete.				
South Atlantic					
22. Delaware	—0.0295 (0.3593)	+0.0038 (0.0840)	+.1187	13.6	.0031
23. Maryland and District of Columbia	—0.9872[aaa] (0.0068)	—0.0036 (0.2676)	+.0264	2.7	.9998[aaa]
24. Virginia	—0.9993[aaa] (0.0088)	+0.0747 (0.1960)	+.0613	6.3	.9997[aaa]
25. West Virginia	—0.9793[aaa] (0.0117)	—0.2508 (0.1401)	+.0737	7.6	.9995[aaa]
26. North and South Carolina	—1.3701 (0.5266)	+1.1013 (3.8283)	—.0549	—5.3	.6831
27. Georgia	—0.9897[aaa] (0.0142)	+0.0234 (0.1871)	+.1006	10.6	.9993[aaa]
28. Florida	—0.9706[aaa] (0.0275)	—0.1873 (0.3102)	+.0815	8.5	.9976[aaa]
East South Central					
29. Kentucky	—1.0300[aaa] (0.0246)	—0.1011 (0.1190)	+.0444	4.5	.9971[aaa]
30. Tennessee	—1.0690[aaa] (0.0389)	+0.5697 (0.4665)	+.0630	6.5	.9969[aaa]
31. Alabama	—0.9802[aaa] (0.0114)	+0.0444 (0.1356)	+.0648	6.7	.9994[aaa]
32. Mississippi	—0.9841[aaa] (0.0371)	+0.0824 (0.1694)	+.0528	5.4	.9947[aaa]

[aaa] Significant at one-tenth of one per cent level.

TABLE 1.4.1 HOUSEHOLD SHORT-RUN REGRESSIONS BY STATES, 1934–41
(continued)

State	α	β	k	Autonomous Growth Rate (per cent)	R^2
West South Central					
33. Arkansas	—1.0085[aaa] (0.0226)	—0.1137 (0.1997)	+.0703	7.3	.9981[aaa]
34. Louisiana	—0.9826[aaa] (0.0249)	—0.2185 (0.3198)	+.0789	8.2	.9992[aaa]
35. Oklahoma	—0.9971[aaa] (0.0136)	—0.2688 (0.1531)	+.0638	6.6	.9992[aaa]
36. Texas	—1.0091[aaa] (0.0031)	+0.1575 (0.0656)	+.0512	5.2	.9999[aaa]
Mountain					
37. Montana	—0.9932[aaa] (0.0154)	—0.1943 (0.1580)	+.0777	8.1	.9990[aaa]
38. Idaho	—0.9801[aaa] (0.0071)	—0.0293 (0.0753)	+.0707	7.3	.9998[aaa]
39. Wyoming	—1.4743[a] (0.3683)	—0.1370 (0.1151)	+.0354	3.6	.7886[a]
40. Colorado	—0.9807[aaa] (0.0178)	—0.1708 (0.1958)	+.0567	5.8	.9992[aaa]
41. New Mexico	Data are incomplete.				
42. Arizona	Data are incomplete.				
43. Utah	—1.0027[aaa] (0.0054)	+0.1109 (0.0548)	+.0385	4.1	.9998[aaa]
44. Nevada	—0.0757 (0.4924)	+0.1858 (0.2222)	+.0966	10.1	.1780
Pacific					
45. Washington	—1.0005[aaa] (0.0071)	+0.0705 (0.1379)	+.0317	3.2	.9998[aaa]
46. Oregon	—0.9994[aaa] (0.0122)	+0.0987 (0.1133)	+.0506	5.2	.9993[aaa]
47. California	—1.0592[aaa] (0.2272)	+0.4568 (0.7203)	—.0418	—4.1	.8569[a]

[a] Significant at five per cent level.
[aaa] Significant at one-tenth of one per cent level.

but correlations as high as this must be due to some other cause. We
have little desire to espouse the position that the lower the correla-

tions, the better are the results, but it seems at least a little unlikely that we have discovered a behavioral pattern with almost no noise elements.

Further grounds for suspicion are afforded us by the magnitudes of the estimates of α. While we shall argue below that it is reasonable that these should all be considerably farther from zero than is the general case in Table 1.3.1, that argument does not imply that the estimates should nearly all be so close to minus one as they are. What makes this particular value so suspect is that a value of minus one for α is what would be obtained if average price fell proportionately with rising electricity consumption for reasons other than those of demand. We should obtain such values if rate schedules were all the same within a state, if they were all two part (or effectively two part, *i.e.*, if all consumers stayed in the same step), with the early step—fixed cost—relatively large, and if there were no variation in the consumer price index. Now, these conditions were not realized in fact. Rate schedules were not all the same, consumers were probably not all in the same step of a multi-step tariff, and there was considerable variation in the consumer price index. It is thus hard to see why our arguments given above as to the possibility of ignoring this problem when using first differences do not apply here.

There is one other possibility, however. The data used to obtain these results were not like the data used for the postwar period as total revenue from residential sales was not given. Instead, figures were provided on revenue per kilowatt hour and on average annual bills. We do not know how these figures were calculated, but we used the former set as prices. If (as seems possible, but unlikely) these figures were not derived from actual revenue figures but were calculated on some reasonable, but more artificial basis, such calculation could result in a relationship such as the one observed.[35] However, even

---

[35] For example, this would be the case if the average annual bills were calculated by averaging the *rate schedules* within a state directly and then computing the average bill by applying the averaged schedule to an estimate of average electricity consumption. This would have the effect of imposing a single rate schedule on each state.

here, it is hard to see why movements in the consumer price index during the thirties would not upset such a relationship, if not entirely, then far more than would be the case if such a relationship is to account for our very high correlation results.

So much for suspicion. From now on we shall not question the gifts of a bountiful Nature, but shall treat them as genuine. The above remarks should be kept in mind throughout, however.

We first look at the autonomous growth rates in the results. It is strikingly clear that they are considerably lower, by and large, than the corresponding growth rates for the postwar period. There the range was from 6.8 per cent to 17.6 per cent; here it is from a *decline* of 5.3 per cent to an increase of 13.6 per cent,[36] with most rates being very low. Of course, this difference reflects a corresponding difference in the rate of growth of population and in the level of long-run income. Nevertheless, the conclusion seems indicated that the introduction of new and different appliances in the postwar period accounted for a good deal of the increased growth rate in those years. We shall return to this at the end of Chapter 3.

Figure 1.4.1 plots α against β as in Figure 1.3.1, with which it should be compared at this time. The difference is striking. Whereas the earlier figure shows a considerable scatter, now we observe that almost all of the points are clustered about the line $\alpha = -1$. There is a moderate tendency to the now familiar rural-urban pattern in the income elasticities of the states of our Groups A-C, with more states than in the postwar period having negative β (as should be expected), but this is dwarfed beside the prevailing tendency toward unitary price elasticity.

This tendency is more interesting. We observed at the end of the last section that the economically younger states in the postwar period tended to have greater price elasticity than the economically older states. This is consistent with our observations here, where all states are economically younger by a considerable amount. In terms of our

---

[36] It is difficult to believe in either extreme here. On the other hand, most of the growth rates observed are quite reasonable.

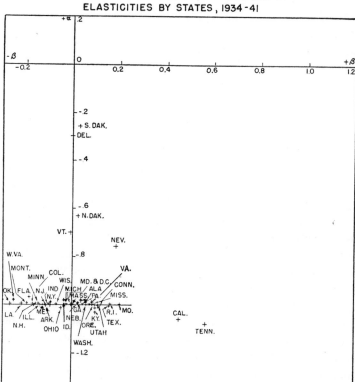

FIG. I.4.I SHORT-RUN PRICE AND INCOME
ELASTICITIES BY STATES, 1934-41

argument as to the formation of habit patterns, it is quite possible
that in the thirties the electricity using habit had not been so strongly formed or so widely spread into different aspects of household
chores that the labor of the housewife was not an unusual substitute
for appliance use in all states, whereas in the forties and fifties such
substitution was unusual in economically older (and richer) states.

To take an example, consider the use of the washing machine. It is a rare housewife who today owns a washing machine and still does the major part of her own wash by hand. When (or where) washers were relatively new, such substitution may have been more common.

Moreover, the substitution of appliance use for personal labor was more likely to be induced by the falling real cost of electricity when incomes were low. We argued in the last section that electricity costs bulk larger in the budget when incomes are low, and there is no need to cite stastistics on the incomes of the thirties. As electricity became relatively cheaper, it became increasingly attractive to learn to substitute the use of an existing appliance for one's own labor.

However, this is not a sufficient argument, by any means, for the variety of appliances widely owned in the thirties was somewhat limited (but recall that farm data are included here). We must argue, in addition to the learning argument just given, that real responses to the cost of electricity in the use of appliances and fixtures did exist at low incomes, that at relatively high costs, the carpet sweeper or the broom was substituted for the vacuum cleaner, that attention was paid to the costs of burning unnecessary light bulbs, and so forth. The incomes of the thirties were low enough to encourage this kind of behavior, and we do not find substantial demand elasticity, although perhaps more than might be expected *a priori*.

Further, it must be repeated that these results are consistent with our results for the postwar period. If the behavior discussed exists below a certain income level, then it is quite plausible to see all states exhibiting it during the Depression and only relatively poorer states exhibiting it after the war (and even these do not exhibit it so strongly). A similar statement holds for the level of economic development and the acquisition of the electricity-using habit.

All this has implications for the future, moreover. We argued from our analysis of the rural-urban difference in the last section that the future would see greater sensitivity in appliance use to short-run income changes. If our (somewhat suspect) results for the prewar period are correct, or if the implications we have drawn from the differences between Groups A-C and Groups D-F in the last section are warranted, it would also appear that the future will see lower sensitivity to the cost of electricity.

Finally, the existence of fairly high short-run price elasticity (either prewar, or in some areas, or both) has moderately interesting policy implications. To these we shall return at the end of Chapter 3.

CHAPTER 2

ESTIMATION OF CONSUMERS' STOCKS BY STATES OF SELECTED MAJOR APPLIANCES, 1944–57

The long-run household demand function for electricity is primarily the demand function for stocks of white goods. In the next chapter we shall discuss that function and its consequences; here we are concerned with the preliminary and vital problem of data.

As already mentioned, adequate time series on white goods stocks by states do not exist. Furthermore, our analysis of the last chapter showed strongly that behavioral differences among regions of the country cannot be ignored.[1] We cannot therefore resort to the use of national aggregates. Fortunately, however, there are some state data available on a selected list of appliances: refrigerators, washing machines, electric ranges, ironing machines, electric clothes dryers, food freezers, electric water heaters, radios, and television sets. The adequacy of such data shows a great range of variation, from very good in the case of refrigerators to very bad in the case of the last few items. In fact, the only available series on sales by states of radios and television sets combines the two goods for three crucial years. We have therefore not attempted construction of state stock series for radios and television sets.

The remainder of this chapter is devoted to a discussion of the available data and our construction procedures for the remaining seven white goods. The results of these efforts are given in Appendix B. All data referred to are from *Electrical Merchandising*[2] and are in numbers of physical units.

---

[1] The same conclusion has been reached by other investigators from budgetary data. See, for example, V. LIPPITT, *Determinants of Consumer Demand for House Furnishings and Equipment*, Cambridge: Harvard University Press, 1959, pp. 59 seq.

[2] A McGraw-Hill publication. We have used the annual statistical issues.

(1) *Refrigerators:* The data available here are estimates of the following: sales by states for 1933–42 and 1946–57; sales nationally for 1945–57 and for as many years before 1942 as necessary for the following procedure;[3] end-of-year stocks by states for 1950 and for all necessary earlier years; end-of-year stocks nationally for all necessary years to the present.

While *Electrical Merchandising's* estimates of end-of-year stocks by states—derived from reports of electric utility companies, for the most part—are undoubtedly open to serious question, it seemed unlikely that we could seriously improve upon them. We therefore accepted those stock estimates, adjusting them where necessary, by multiplying each of them by the ratio of the national estimate to the total of state estimates to ensure compatibility. It remained to estimate end-of-year stocks by states for 1951–57.

To do this, it was first necessary to generate sales by state figures for 1945. Sales were zero in 1943 and 1944. (We give a general description as the same procedure had to be followed for some other years in the case of other white goods.) This was done in the following manner: estimated national stocks at the end of year $t - 1$ were subtracted from estimated national stocks at the end of year t. This difference—the net change in national stocks during year t—must be equal to national sales less depreciation (scrapping or trade-ins) during year t. Accordingly, the net change in national stocks during year

---

[3] Actually, *Electrical Merchandising* gives two different series on national sales, both here and for some other white goods for those years in which sales by states are given. Neither series is always quite the total of state sales for some goods and there is no large or systematic difference between them, for the most part. We have used the series given with the state sales, where available, and have troubled neither with the difference between the two series nor with the adjustment of the state sales figures to ensure that they add to the national figures. Such adjustments would have been very minor; moreover, since we ultimately adjust our state *stock* estimates to ensure their totalling to the national *stock* estimates given by *Electrical Merchandising*, they are ultimately roughly made implicitly, in any case. Besides, as usual, systematic proportional errors will be eliminated in the analysis of the next chapter. Note that we have no way of testing the quality of these sales estimates, which is probably low for the state series.

t was subtracted from national sales in year t to obtain an estimate of such depreciation. The resulting figure was then divided by the estimated national stock at the end of year $t-1$ to obtain an estimate of the percentage depreciation of the latter stock. It was then assumed that the same percentage depreciation of the stock at the end of year $t-1$ applied during year t in every state separately. Total depreciation during year t was accordingly calculated for each state, and this was added to the change in estimated end-of-year stocks during year t to obtain estimated state sales in that year.

Now, the assumption involved in the above—that percentage depreciation in year t was the same in all states—is, of course, a bad one. Indeed, we refuse to make it or any similar assumption where it counts— in actually estimating state stocks—and thus to make our task far lighter. Here, however, such an assumption is relatively minor. State sales are by far the major part of net changes in state stocks. Moreover, the estimated sales for the early years only enter into our ultimate estimates as affecting the age distribution of the various state stocks. This is somewhat true even for 1945, and here total sales were, of course, very small. The errors introduced into our final results by making the uniform depreciation assumption at this stage are therefore negligible.

Having now a complete series of sales figures, we proceeded as follows. We assumed that, for a community sufficiently homogeneous, the refrigerators scrapped or traded in during a given year are always the oldest in existence. We further made the negligible assumption that sales of refrigerators are spread evenly throughout the year.[4] As our first approximation, we assumed that the United States as a whole was sufficiently homogeneous, in the above sense. For each year, beginning with 1951, therefore, we cumulated estimated national sales backwards in time until their total equaled estimated

---

[4] This is negligible partly because it is only needed for the early years— generally, the years before World War II. It would be untrue for 1950, for example, when sales of appliances rose sharply in the second half of the year owing to the Korean War. Even if we had to apply the even spreading of sales assumption here, however, its ultimate effects could be neglected.

national end-of-year stock for the year in question. The time elapsed from the earliest date reached in this process to the end of the year of the stock estimate was then taken as an estimate of the age of the oldest existing refrigerator at the latter time.

An easy, but woefully inadequate assumption would now have been that the age of the oldest existing unit in each state was equal to this estimated age, so that the desired state stock estimates would be similar cumulations of state sales estimates. The difficulty with this assumption is that there are in fact systematic differences among regions of the country in the age of the oldest existing unit of a given appliance (what we shall call, for convenience, "scrapping age"). These differences are greater for some other appliances than for refrigerators, but they can never be ignored. In general, going through the above procedure for each state separately for 1950 (the last year for which outside state stock estimates were available) revealed that the Northeast tends to have older stocks than the rest of the country, and the Southeast younger. For washing machines, for example, state estimates of scrapping age varied from roughly six years in some southern states to roughly eighteen years in parts of New England. The reason for this effect is probably that the Southern states were only able to purchase adequate equipment for the first time after the great rise in incomes experienced during the war, and that electrification was relatively late in the South.

Furthermore, it is not sufficient to argue that the effects of this kind of difference will disappear because, for example, excessive backward cumulation of sales will add very little to the stock estimates in southern states, where sales were very low before the war. Although that argument is correct, the large bias would come in the estimates for the Northeast, where uncritical adoption of a national scrapping age estimate would lead to systematic underestimation of stocks as backward cumulation of sales estimates would not go far enough. All in all, we must improve on our first approximation. Fortunately, the means are at hand to do this.

As our second approximation, we assumed that the ratio of the scrapping age estimate for each state to the scrapping age estimate for the country as a whole was the same for all later years as for 1950.[5] For each later year, the age of the oldest existing unit in each state was obtained using this assumption. These resulting estimated ages were accepted as final estimates, unless they were such as to place the date of acquisition of the oldest unit later than the start of 1945, in which case our third and final approximation was applied. For such cases (and indeed, for 1950 stocks where the same difficulty arose) the start of 1945 was used as a starting date, save in the case of the national estimate of the earliest date of acquisition falling later than 1945 (which only happened for 1957 and in the case of water heaters, below). In this latter case, the first approximation of equal scrapping ages in all states was applied.[6]

In essence, then, we assumed a constant differential over states in the matter of scrapping age, adjusting this assumption by further assuming that no postwar-sold refrigerators were scrapped until all prewar-sold ones had disappeared. Preliminary estimates of state stocks were then obtained as cumulated state sales from the estimated time of acquisition of the oldest unit. This method, like any other, no doubt leaves much to be desired; it seems doubtful that it could be much improved upon, however, given the primary data available.

Fortunately, one check, if only a very rough one, is available to us. While the use of the crude and incorrect first approximation of equal

---

[5] This seemed slightly better than did a similar assumption in terms of the differences between state and national scrapping age estimates. The fact that 1950 was the first year of the Korean War is beside the point. Provided that the effect of the war scare on scrapping and replacement acted in each state in the same relative way as did all other factors affecting these things, there is no reason not to use it. Furthermore, 1950 is the last year for which state stock estimates were available. Using it in this way thus provided the best estimates of relative scrapping age by states just before our general procedure had to be applied. To have used any earlier year would have been to run the risk of concluding that the oldest existing refrigerator in some state at the end of 1951 had been sold before the date of sale of the oldest existing refrigerator in the same state at the end of 1950.

[6] There was one later exception to this. For some appliances, application of the second (constant-ratio) approximation for 1957 yielded dates of earliest acquisition in one or two states before 1943. These dates were accepted instead of the national average date. This was a rare occurrence, however.

scrapping ages throughout would have ensured that our estimates totaled to the national stock estimates of *Electrical Merchandising* (save for rounding error), no such result was built into our figures. Our estimates were thus finally adjusted by multiplying each of them by the ratio of the national stock estimates to their total to ensure compatibility with the national series. While an adjustment factor of unity is, of course, compatible with all sorts of horrendous but cancelling errors in the figures for individual states, and while the fact that we start our process with the national estimate of scrapping age means that we are unlikely to be wildly off in our totals, it is nevertheless reassuring to note that our adjustment factors are all very close to one—closer, in fact, than the similar adjustment factors for some of *Electrical Merchandising*'s own state stock estimates for earlier years—and that no strong trend appears in them so that no large systematic errors are present in the totals. The final adjustment factors for all appliances are presented in Table 2.1.1.

(2) *Washing Machines:* The same data as for refrigerators are available here and state sales go back to 1932. The data were sometimes given separately (nationally) for automatic and semi-automatic washers on the one hand, and conventional, wringer-type washers on the other. Where necessary, we combined the two.

(3) *Electric Ranges:* Here the data are less complete than in the former two cases. While essentially the same national series are given, there are no state series of either sales or end-of-year stocks for years before 1939.[7] Furthermore, stock estimates for all years are given only for the total of Delaware and Maryland and the District of Columbia, and separate sales estimates for those states start only with 1947.

We treated these problems as follows. First, the two missing states were treated as a unit in applying the procedures already described, and yearly stock estimates were derived for them. These estimates, while given in Appendix B, were not used in our analysis below; they were merely used in calculating the final adjustment factors.

As for state sales before 1939, we assumed that the proportion of

---

[7] State sales estimates for 1942 had to be secured by the method described above.

national sales in each state was the same in earlier years as in the total sales for 1939–42 (because of demonstration effects and the like). This assumption, while not good, seems the best available. Its adoption means that the state stock estimates for ranges are somewhat less reliable than for refrigerators or washing machines. However, the goodness of the final adjustment factors (Table 2.1.1) leads us to believe that the errors involved may be minor.

(4) *Ironing Machines:* The data here are the same as for refrigerators back to 1939. Unfortunately, however, the life of these goods appears to be so long that state sales for many earlier years are needed, especially in Idaho and Wyoming, for our procedures to be applied. National sales are available back to 1925 and thus far we assumed that state to national sales ratios were the same as for the totals for 1939–42. Before 1925, however, we were forced to guess at national sales, and we set them always equal to 1925 sales. This, however, could not be right, for applying it made stocks in Idaho and Wyoming in 1950 date back before the turn of the century. We therefore arbitrarily cut off state sales estimates in 1900, assuming that all remaining unaccounted-for units were sold in that year. Again, this is all wrong but our final adjustment factors indicate that we may be right in thinking it makes little difference in the end result. Remember, what is at issue here is not the size but the precise age distribution of the 1950 state stocks. Errors here, so long as they are not too large, will not overly affect the end results, although, of course, they are not desirable. Our figures for ironing machines are thus probably not too bad, although they are not of comparable reliability with those for the first two white goods discussed or even with those for electric ranges.

(5) *Electric Clothes Dryers:* Here national sales data begin with 1947; state sales data with 1947; and national stock figures with 1948. There are no data on state stocks for any year.

The procedure followed here was somewhat different from that used for the first four white goods. First, national sales for 1948 and 1947 were subtracted from national end-of-year stock for 1948 to obtain an estimate of the national end-of-year stock of 1946 still existing at the end of 1948. It was then assumed that no depreciation took place between 1946 and 1948 so that this estimate was considered an estimate of the actual national end-of-year stock for 1946. This assumption is not a bad one, as dryers in existence at the end of 1946 were mostly postwar, few dryers having been manufactured before the war. In any case, the national end-of-year stock thus estimated for 1946 was small relative to later sales, so that errors here are not large in the final results.

Next, we split this estimated national figure among the various states by assuming that the proportion in each state was the same here as for sales during 1947.

Finally, state end-of-year stocks for 1947–57 were estimated by making our first crude approximation discussed above. That is, for each year beginning with 1947 we found the number of years' sales (starting with the latest possible) and proportion of the 1946 end-of-year stock that were required to give the national end-of-year stock for that year. The same years' sales and proportion of 1946 end-of-year stock were then added for every state. The usual final adjustment factors were employed, but we do not present them below since, save for rounding error and inconsistent reporting by *Electrical Merchandising*,[8] the procedure just described ensures that they are all unity.

The assumption used here—our first approximation—is probably better here and below in the case of food freezers than it would have been in the case of the first four white goods discussed. This is so be-

---

[8] One case which we believe to be inconsistent reporting should be noted here. (Others will be given for food freezers below.) The sales figures given by *Electrical Merchandising* for 1954 for Utah and Nevada are clearly wrong by comparison with 1953 and 1955. We have assumed that the figures for the two states were inadvertently switched, with the Utah figure given for Nevada and *vice versa*. A plausible but very slightly less likely explanation would be that only the first digits of each number were reversed. Fortunately, adopting this assumption would have given approximately the same result as that actually obtained. Whatever the exact truth may be, it is clear that some such error was made as the 1954 figures are way out of line for the state for which they are given and about what one would expect for the other state. "*Natura non facit saltum.*"

cause we are not applying it to prewar stocks and sales. We said above that such sales were likely to be the ones where the approximation in question was least good.

(6) *Food Freezers:* Here the situation is much like that in the case of clothes dryers and essentially the same techniques were employed. The only major difference is that state sales figures do not begin until 1948. We thus split both national end-of-year stocks in 1946 and national sales in 1947 in the same proportions among the states as national sales in 1948. There is probably greater error involved here than in the case of clothes dryers, however, as food freezer sales before the war were not negligible. For the same reason as is given above, final adjustment factors are not presented for this white good.[9]

(7) *Electric Water Heaters:* Here the truly heroic assumption must be called into play, for here the data are very incomplete. National sales estimates go back well before the war, but state sales estimates only begin with 1947 and there are no state end-of-year stock estimates.

The principal difficulty here is twofold—how to split up national sales before 1947 among the states, and how to take account of different scrapping ages in different states. As to the first problem, we might have adopted a procedure similar to that used previously and assumed that state sales before the war were proportional to state sales in the postwar period. The argument for this would have been that state sales after the war were principally replacement sales. This

---

[9] One difficulty of inconsistent reporting must be mentioned here. It twice occurs that estimated national end-of-year stocks as given by *Electrical Merchandising* for the year $t-1$ plus estimated national sales for year t are less than estimated national end-of-year stocks for year t. This, of course, is impossible in reality and the reports are inconsistent. It is difficult to know which estimate is wrong or whether all of them are and just what to do about this. Any adjustment would be arbitrary. We decided to adjust the figures by looking at estimated scrapping age for the years immediately around the year for which the difficulty occurred and changing that year for which scrapping age seemed out of line by making its scrapping age the average of the two scrapping ages for the years immediately before and after it and recalculating the national stock estimate accordingly. This changed the national end-of-year stock estimate for 1948 by $+6.73$ per cent and the national end-of-year stock estimate for 1953 by -1.18 per cent. Fortunately, these adjustments affect only the given year; their effects are not cumulative.

would not have been a valid argument, however. Nor would an argument from demonstration effects have been convincing, for the character of the appliance market changed greatly due to the great rise in incomes during the war. This was particularly true in southern states where electrification conditions were also rapidly changing. It is thus clear that the simplest assumption will not work here.

Another, perhaps better, assumption is available, however. Electric water heaters are and were subject to strong substitute competition—principally from gas-fired water heaters. To a large extent, before the war, regions which had relatively available and cheap gas probably tended to be regions with relatively few electric water heaters. A similar statement, however, applies to electric ranges where gas competition is and was also very important. Furthermore, the use of either an electric range or an electric water heater means arranging and paying for heavy duty household power lines. To an extent, especially when incomes were low before the war, we should expect gas ranges and gas water heaters to go together and electric ranges and electric water heaters to go together. This tendency is by no means universal, but it is probably correct to say that states which had or bought a lot of electric ranges, relatively, probably also had or bought a lot of electric water heaters, relatively. We therefore split national sales of electric water heaters for prewar years among the states in the same proportions as sales of electric ranges (see above). For 1945 and 1946, we split national sales in the same proportions as for 1947.

We can go further than this, however. We assumed that *relative* scrapping ages over states were the same for electric water heaters as for electric ranges, differences in the durability of the two goods being the same for all states. The idea here is that the influences on scrapping age should be just about the same—gas competition being the chief factor—for both white goods for a given state. Over-all differences in scrapping age, as stated, are not affected by this assumption but are independently estimated by means of the national end-of-year stock figures.

One further difficulty remains. *Electrical Merchandising* gives national end-of-year stock estimates for 1945 and 1947–57 but gives no such estimate for 1946. We therefore constructed such an estimate by interpolation as follows: we subtracted the net change in estimated national end-of-year stocks from 1945 to 1947 from total estimated national sales for 1946 and 1947 to obtain estimated national depreciation of the 1945 end-of-year stock during 1946 and 1947. Estimated national depreciation of that stock during 1946 was then taken as the same fraction of this latter estimate as sales during 1946 were of total sales in the two years. This is probably not unreasonable. Given estimated national depreciation during 1946, estimated national end-of-year stock for that year was then easily constructed using estimated national end-of-year stock for 1945.

It will be readily apparent from all this that our water heater figures are rather largely guesses. However, the final adjustment figures obtained once more indicate that the guesses may not be wildly wrong.

TABLE 2.1.1 FINAL ADJUSTMENT FACTORS: FIVE WHITE GOODS

	Year	Final Adjustment Factor[a]
Refrigerators	1951	0.9970
	1952	0.9961
	1953	1.0033
	1954	1.0032
	1955	0.9979
	1956	0.9986
	1957	0.9944
Washing Machines	1947	0.9469[b]
	1948	0.9501[b]
	1949	0.9527[b]
	1950	0.9564[b]
	1951	0.9970
	1952	0.9947
	1953	0.9953
	1954	1.0043

[a] Equals ratio of estimated national end-of-year stock to total of state estimates at last stage (see text). A value of unity means no adjustment necessary.
[b] Adjustment of *Electrical Merchandising* state end-of-year stock estimates. These figures are presented for comparative purposes.

TABLE 2.1.1 FINAL ADJUSTMENT FACTORS: FIVE WHITE GOODS

(continued)

	Year	Final Adjustment Factor[a]
Washing Machines	1955	1.0064
(continued)	1956	0.9849
	1957	1.0076[c]
Electric Ranges	1951	1.0033
	1952	1.0048
	1953	1.0060
	1954	1.0054
	1955	0.9846
	1956	0.9841
	1957	0.9965[c]
Ironing Machines	1951	1.0008
	1952	1.0022
	1953	1.0030
	1954	1.0028
	1955	1.0046
	1956	1.0063
	1957	1.0082
Electric Water Heaters	1945	1.0031
	1946	0.9966
	1947	1.0012
	1948	1.0019
	1949	1.0036
	1950	1.0010
	1951	0.9909
	1952	1.0008[c]
	1953	1.0008[c]
	1954	0.9995[c]
	1955	0.9995[c]
	1956	0.9996[c]
	1957	1.0002[c]

[a] Equals ratio of estimated national end-of-year stock to total of state estimates at last stage (see text). A value of unity means no adjustment necessary.
[b] Adjustment of *Electrical Merchandising* state end-of-year stock estimates. These figures are presented for comparative purposes.
[c] Rounding errors only. Presented for comparative purposes.

CHAPTER 3

ELECTRICITY DEMAND BY HOUSEHOLDS: THE LONG RUN

1. The Model: Alternative Specifications

Chapter 1 was concerned with the characteristics of electricity demand by households in the short run—that is, with the demand for electricity with the stock of electricity-using appliances assumed given. Now we must turn to the more important question of the long-run characteristics of household demand, to the demand for white goods themselves. In particular, we shall be interested in the question—generally ignored by writers on the demand for durables—of the effects of the price of electricity and of the price of gas on the demand for major appliances (as well as on the number of wired households) rather than in a complete and satisfactory analysis of all aspects of appliance demand. Should it turn out that the price of electricity has no effect on any component of the stock of white goods, we shall conclude that the analysis of the first chapter probably said all that there is to say about the price elasticity of electricity demand by households. On the other hand, should we find such effects, then these must be combined with our former results. In any case, after completing this part of our analysis, we shall be in a position to evaluate the characteristics of the total demand by households, both long- and short-run.

It is very tempting to use a stock adjustment model that is a slight variant of a familiar type. In a slight change from the first chapter, let W_{it} denote the stock of the ith white good possessed by the community at the end of the tth time period. *In this chapter, we drop the convention, earlier adopted, of measuring all white good stocks in kilowatt-hours-per-hour-of-normal-use units, unless otherwise noted.* The W_{it} are therefore in physical units. (We shall worry about the problem of quality changes over time below.) We define W_{it}^e as the equilibrium value of W_{it}, that is, W_{it}^e is the stock of white goods which households would eventually hold if all the variables which influence their desires were to maintain the values which they have in the tth period for an infinite time.

The familiar linear stock adjustment model is:

$$(3.1.1) \qquad W_{it} - W_{it-1} = \varrho_i(W^e_{it} - W_{it-1})$$

where $1 \geq \varrho_i > 0$. The usual interpretation of this equation is that households adjust their stocks during period t by a constant fraction of the difference between the stocks they start with and their desired equilibrium stocks. This is a finite approximation to the differential equation:

$$(3.1.1') \qquad dW_i/dt = \varrho_i(W^e_{it} - W_{it})$$

so that the speed of adjustment in stocks is made proportional to the "stress"—that is, to the difference between desired and actual stocks.[1] $\varrho_i = 1$ means complete adjustment during a single time period. Of course, if W^e_{it} remains constant over time, it is approached asymptotically by W_{it}.

Now, a different model of the same genus, namely the logarithmic variant of the above, would seem more convenient for our purposes. There is little *a priori* reason to prefer one variant of the model rather than the other, and since W^e_{it} is made a power function of various variables below, the following assumption would be more convenient than is (3.1.1):

$$(3.1.2) \qquad \log W_{it} - \log W_{it-1} = \varrho_i(\log W^e_{it} - \log W_{it-1})$$

where, as before, $1 \geq \varrho i > 0$. This is, of course, equivalent to:

$$(3.1.3) \qquad \frac{W_{it}}{W_{it-1}} = \left(\frac{W^e_{it}}{W_{it-1}}\right)^{\varrho_i}.$$

---

[1] Examples of the use of models of this general type are too numerous to list in detail. A recent example of the logarithmic variant about to be described is J. R. N. STONE AND D. A. ROWE, "The Market Demand for Durable Goods," *Econometrica*, 25 (July, 1957), No. 3, pp. 423–43. Such models have even been applied to the demand for agricultural commodities by M. NERLOVE AND W. ADDISON, "Statistical Estimation of Long-Run Elasticities of Supply and Demand," *Journal of Farm Economics*, XL (November, 1958), No. 4, pp. 861–80.

Here it is the ratio, rather than the difference of stocks that is adjusted. Completion of the model would now require only discussion of the truly substantive question of the determinants of W_{it}^e. As this question must be discussed regardless of the model used, we now consider it.

Those determinants are dishearteningly many. They probably include among others: at least one appropriate income variable; the price of the white good; the price of any gas-using substitute; the price of electricity and the average electricity consumption of the white good; the price of gas if a gas-using substitute exists; the number of wired households per capita and the size of population; some variable to represent the average age of households. We now discuss some of these.

No matter what view of the theory of consumer behavior one takes, it seems clear that the purchase of a major appliance does not depend solely on current income. Such purchases generally require some previous accumulation of savings. Alternatively, one might plausibly argue that white good purchases are planned in advance so that the income out of which durables are purchased is expected, permanent income, rather than temporary current windfalls.[2] Since such permanent income is usually measured by a moving average of past incomes, and since accumulated saving, whether or not it depends on permanent income as such, certainly depends on such a moving average, these two views are much the same for our purposes. Since limitations on the availability of data on personal assets by states make it impossible for us to include that variable explicitly, we shall use an income variable, $Y_t{}^E$, which is a moving average of real personal income per capita.[3] In particular, we shall use a seventeen-year average with the weights provided by Friedman in his analysis of the

---

[2] See FRIEDMAN, *op. cit.*, and F. MODIGLIANI AND R. BRUMBERG, "Utility Analysis and the Consumption Function: An Interpretation of Cross-Section Data," in *Post-Keynesian Economics* (K. KURIHARA, ed.), New Brunswick: Rutgers University Press, 1954, pp. 388–436. This sort of theory seems strongest when it comes to the demand for durables.

[3] Per capita, because population will also be included.

consumption function.[4] (While there are seventeen years involved, the weights decline exponentially as we recede from year t so that the total weight attached to income in year t and the four years immediately preceding it is 86.5 per cent of the sum of the weights.) This decision is greatly strengthened by the successful use of the same variable by G. Chow in his study of the demand for automobiles.[5]

There seems no need to discuss the use of the price of the white good or the price of its gas-using substitute, if any. We represent these by E_{it} and G_{it} respectively and measure them in real terms.

We now turn to a discussion of the role of the price of electricity and of the white good's power requirements. It seems clear that, at least in the case where a gas-using substitute appliance is available, the cost of operating an electric appliance may enter into the decision to purchase it. Even where new gas appliances are relatively unimportant substitutes, as in the case of refrigerators, the running cost may enter into the decision of when an existing gas appliance should be replaced. It is further possible, although less likely, that operating costs enter into demand even where no gas-using substitute exists, because of the availability of substitutes outside the home for the services of the white good or because of the availability of the household's own labor or the services of domestics. The first factor might be expected to operate most strongly in urban states; the second, which is becoming increasingly less important, might be expected to apply in the South.

Now, for a fixed C_i of the first chapter, the average number of hours of use of a unit of the appliance, the expected cost of operation can be represented by $\gamma_{it}P_t^E$, where P_t^E is the expected real price of electricity per kilowatt hour (measured by means of a three-year moving average) and γ_{it} is the kilowatt hour consumption of a new unit of the appliance per hour of average use. However, the use of such a product in our analysis presents some analytical difficulties.

---

[4] FRIEDMAN, *op. cit.*, p. 147. Some minor details of the construction of this average will be given in the next section.

[5] G. CHOW, *Demand for Automobiles in the United States*, Amsterdam: North-Holland Publishing Co., 1957.

If we only used a variable representing the cost of an hour's use of the appliance in question, we would find that such a variable could change in two ways—through a change in electricity price, and through a change in normal kilowatt hour consumption. It is at the least not obvious that such changes have equivalent effects on the desired equilibrium stock of the appliance, for the first affects the operating costs of existing and new appliances in equal proportions, whereas the second affects only the operating costs of new units. We should therefore expect the influence of a change in normal kilowatt hour consumption to be of two kinds as it might affect the timing of replacement purchases as well as influencing the non-replacement demand. Further, changes in γ_{it} are to some extent the results of quality changes. We therefore use γ_{it} and P_t^E as separate variables in our analysis.

Similar remarks apply to the use of V_t^E, a three-year moving average of gas prices. Here, however, we shall have to be content with assuming the number of therms per hour of normal use used by a given appliance to be constant, as information on the matter is difficult to come by.

Now, it is clear that there is a complementary relationship between the wiring of a household and the use of electric appliances therein. We must therefore use some measure of the number of wired households as a variable. It would be possibly erroneous, however, to make the tempting assumption that appliance demand varies directly with the number of wired households. If that is so, we shall find it in the results, but it need not be the case. In poorer states not every household is wired. The number of wired households per capita is therefore an index of the state of development—of the general living standard. Alternatively, the demand for appliances depends not simply upon the mean of the expected income distribution, but also upon other parameters thereof. In particular, it may well be the case that some minimum income is required for the household to have any interest in such purchases. Even if that minimum is above the minimum required to wire the household, the number of wired households per capita provides some measure of what proportion of the state's population is in extremely low income brackets. Further, it is certainly possible that households newly wired have different demand characteristics than do households in which electricity-using habits have been long established.

It is thus not clear that the equilibrium stock of each white good is directly proportional to the number of electricity customers when the good is not near saturation. We therefore use two variables, namely, the number of customers per capita and population. Again, if the kind of effect which we have discussed is not present, both variables will have the same coefficient below. We let H_t represent the first variable and F_t represent the second. We shall later be concerned with the question of whether the price of electricity affects H_t.

Now, we have argued that H_t is an index of living standards. But a demographic variable, also, is called for in our analysis. It is a matter of observation (at least every June) that newly-formed households tend to purchase or be given appliances. Since there has been no over-supply of housing in the United States, this effect even holds true for appliances supplied by landlords, since the setting up of a new household generally means the occupancy of a new dwelling unit somewhere. We therefore use the variable M_t, the average number of marriages in the tth and $t-$ 1st time periods.

The model which would be most convenient to use is linear in the logarithms of all variables as this is simple and as similar models have met with some success elsewhere,[6] and, as such a form would enable us to test the hypothesis that γ_{it} and P_t^E or H_t and F_t have the same effect. Letting primes denote natural logarithms and A be a constant, we have:

$$(3.1.4) \quad W_{it}^{E\prime} = A_i + \eta_{i1} Y_t^{E\prime} + \eta_{i2} E_{it}' + (\eta_{i3} G_{it}') + \eta_{i4}\gamma_{it}' + \eta_{i5} P_t^{E\prime}$$
$$+ (\eta_{i6} V_t^{E\prime}) + \eta_{i7} H_t' + \eta_{i8} M_t' + \eta_{i9} F_t'$$

where the terms in parentheses only appear if a significant gas-using

---

[6] For example, in STONE AND ROWE, op. cit.

substitute exists. When substituted in (3.1.2), this yields:

$$(3.1.5) \quad W'_{it} = \varrho_i A_i + \varrho_i \eta_{i1} Y_t^{E\prime} + \varrho_i \eta_{i2} E_{it} + (\varrho_i \eta_{i3} G_{it}) + \varrho_i \eta_{i4} \gamma'_{it}$$
$$+ \varrho_i \eta_{i5} P_t^{E\prime} + (\varrho_i \eta_{i6} V_t^{E\prime}) + \varrho_i \eta_{i7} H'_t + \varrho_i \eta_{i8} M'_t$$
$$+ \varrho_i \eta_{i9} F'_t + (\mathbf{1} - \varrho_i) W'_{it-1} .$$

Estimation of this equation would thus yield both "short-term" and "long-term" elasticities of the demand for white good stocks,[7] the former being ϱ_i times the latter.

Now, unfortunately, despite its apparent plausibility and fairly widespread success, the stock adjustment model of (3.1.2)—(3.1.5) is entirely unsuited to our purposes. Indeed, its use leads to entirely uninterpretable results as (whether first differences are used or not) W'_{it-1} takes up all variation in W'_{it}. However, a discussion of its defects will lead us directly into the central problems of the present analysis.

Most—perhaps all—past uses of the stock adjustment model have used data which had the property that continuous variability in the stock held by any one individual was reasonably possible. In general, models of this type have been applied to investment in all durables and the like.[8] In such cases, it was not unreasonable to assume that adjustments of actual to desired stock were proportional (either simply or in the logarithms) to the distance between the two. However, our analysis is concerned with the stock of certain physical units; units, moreover, which have the property that a given household gen-

---

[7] We use these adjectives rather than "short-" and "long-run" to avoid confusion with the elasticities of the demand for electricity itself for which we reserve the latter terms.

[8] *E.g.*, STONE AND ROWE, *op. cit.* Most authors use stock measured in value terms as dependent variable. Z. GRILICHES, "The Demand for a Durable Input: Farm Tractors in the United States, 1921–57," in *The Demand for Durable Goods* (A. C. HARBERGER, ed.), Chicago: University of Chicago Press, 1960, does use a physical quantity measure as well. Incidentally, the other studies in this volume (which appeared just before the present book went to press) are all in terms of national aggregates which may help to explain the discrepancy between their results and those reported below.

erally owns one of them at most. Net changes in that stock, therefore, come about overwhelmingly by the purchase of new units by households not previously owning one. While it is true, of course, that the demonstration effects of other households' possessions may influence such purchases, it is unreasonable to use a model which makes such purchases proportional to the difference between desired and actual stock. The actual stock that counts here is zero and the fact that other households in the economic aggregate being considered own the good already is not relevant in this place. To put it another way, however his neighbors' possessions may influence a man's desires, he certainly does not satisfy his own white goods desires by a constant percentage of the difference between them and the average holding in the community; he looks at his own actual stock. In cases which are such that the stock held by an individual can vary more or less continuously over some range, each individual can be assumed to hold the average stock. In cases such as the present one, however, there is no doubt that the individuals doing the purchasing hold a stock of zero, in general. Thus a stock adjustment model is inappropriate here.[9]

What then is an appropriate model? We shall use what can best be described as a "disease" model of the growth of appliance stocks. Here the possession of a unit of the given appliance is considered as the state of having a contagious disease. How many people have the disease at any given time is considered to depend on how many people had it before, how many people there are who are not immune, and on various other factors all affecting susceptibility.

In detail, consider the ratio of W_{tt} to W_{tt-1}. This is a measure of the rate of growth of the disease—of its infectiousness, so to speak. We take this as our dependent variable and consider the effects thereon of various other variables, in general, those already discussed. This specification makes demonstration effects constant relative to the

---

[9] It might be supposed that some sort of aggregate stock adjustment relation does hold, nevertheless, in terms of all white goods owned by the household taken together. While some argument for this can be made, inclusion of white good stocks other than the one for which demand is being explained does not seem to change the results or to be particularly helpful.

size of the stock. Other things being equal, the number of people owning the good this year is proportional to the number owning it last year. The *relative* strength of the effect—of the infectiousness of the disease—varies with other variables, but not with the size of the stock itself. Thus the probability of being infected goes up with exposure, but is only proportional thereto.

Now, how many people have the disease (own the white good) at any given time depends on how many people there are who are not immune to the disease. People can be immune to the white good disease if their households are not wired, if their long-run income position is too low, or—obviously—if they do not exist. W_{tt} therefore depends on H_t, F_t, and on the number of households above a certain minimum permanent income level. It follows that the ratio of W_{tt} to W_{it-1} depends on H_t/H_{t-1}, on F_t/F_{t-1} (as before, we separate these two variables), and on the percentage change in the number of households above the minimum income threshold.

The measurement of the last named variable is difficult. For simplicity, we make the following assumptions: first, the slope of the frequency distribution of permanent incomes is low in the neighborhood of the threshold point; second, over time, the entire income distribution shifts upward together. These assumptions are probably good approximations for the postwar period, since the threshold point can be expected to fall on the lower tail of the income distribution. If they are valid, then the number of persons passing the threshold point in any given year is measured by the movement of mean permanent income. If changes in mean income are small relative to mean income itself, and changes in the number of people above threshold income are small relative to that number, then percentage changes in mean income will roughly measure percentage changes in the number of persons above the threshold. We thus use Y_t^E/Y_{t-1}^E as a variable. This is admittedly a crude and somewhat unsatisfactory approximation, but no better one seems readily available. We shall have to be careful in interpreting the results as regards this variable.

However, even if the above treatment were entirely satisfactory, we should still need another income variable. The threshold concept refers to immunity to the white good disease; we must consider susceptibility. Here the level of, rather than the change in income is important. Further, current, rather than permanent income seems called for. A constant number of households may be able to afford a given white good, yet they may not all own it or even buy it immediately. Other purchases may take precedence or may at least compete with this one. The strength of the desire for the white good—and hence the net change in the stocks thereof—will thus depend on a number of other variables. Among these others will be the level of current income. At high current incomes, competing purchases may have already been made. Moreover, the pressure of the demonstration effect may be greater than at low incomes, as high income families tend to come more in contact with others who own the white good than do low income families. Possession of the white good consequently becomes less special and the good tends to be thought of as more of a necessity with a high living standard. Finally, and perhaps most importantly, with a high current income, a household can readily meet the down payment on an appliance without dipping into past savings or saving for the future. The decision tends to be to buy while the good times last. The argument can be restated as follows: households with high permanent incomes tend to *own* rather than to *buy* appliances, since appliances are durable goods. That is, the demand for appliances is primarily a demand for the services of a *stock* rather than for a flow of appliances. If all permanent incomes were constant, ultimately, other things being equal, the stock of appliances would remain constant and would be greater the higher the income level (up to a saturation point). Net changes in the stock would be zero. It is changes in permanent income which, by changing the desire to own the good, cause people to acquire the stock. On the other hand, the *timing* of acquisitions—and the strength of the desire to own the good—varies with the current income level. Other things being equal, the probability of acquiring a new unit of the appliance this year rather than later is greater the higher is current income. We therefore use Y_t, current income per capita, explicitly in our analysis.

It should now be clear what role is played by appliance prices in the disease-infectiousness model of appliance demand. Like current income, they affect the susceptibility. At high prices, the attractiveness of new appliances is lower than at low ones—the infectiousness of the disease is lower, other things being equal, and it is thus easier to resist catching it. It is clear, moreover, that the consequent view that the effects of appliance prices apply to changes in stocks rather than to the holding of stocks themselves is the correct one. The decision to purchase rather than the decision to hold an appliance is affected by the price thereof. The situation might be otherwise were there a well developed second-hand market in appliances, but this is not the case. In the real world, once an appliance is bought, later prices cease to be of interest (save as indications of virtual capital gain or loss in view of opportunity costs) until the decision for replacement is to be made. We thus include E_{it} rather than percentage changes therein in our analysis. For similar reasons, we include G_{it}, where relevant.

The situation as regards the cost of running the appliance is much the same. Once the appliance is purchased, running costs only affect decisions concerning whether to replace when the appliance is old—not directly the decision to hold an already acquired appliance in good working order. Of course, if the running costs on new models are well below those on old, this may affect the timing of replacements, but this effect is not one that concerns the net change in stocks. Basically, expected running costs at the time of purchase affect the decision to acquire rather than the decision to hold. We therefore include P_t^E, γ_{it}, and, where relevant, V_t^E.

There remains M_t, the number of marriages. In terms of our disease model, we may say that the reason for including this variable is as follows. Unlike the first six months of life, when the infant is immune from many later diseases, the first six months or so of married life are a time of very high susceptibility indeed to the appliance disease. Indeed, this disease—in one or more of its many forms—is often given to the newly formed household by others. M_t is therefore an indication of how many people are in this dangerously susceptible state at a given time.

We have now discussed all the variables that will be included in our model. It is necessary, however, to discuss the omission of another variable, quality change. It certainly seems that some variable representing change in quality should be included. The higher the quality of the appliance, the more attractive it is and the more infectious the disease. Furthermore, if no allowance is made for quality changes and retail prices are used, actual price will in some sense be overstated in the later years of the period studied. On the other hand, quality change is a very difficult thing to measure; moreover, it is not clear what the correct thing to measure is. Just as we use real rather than money prices to remove movements in the general price level from the price variable, so we ought to use what we may term "real" quality changes rather than apparent ones; that is, we should use quality changes corrected for general quality changes in all other goods. Quality improvements in an appliance only contribute to its relative attractiveness if, however measured, they are greater than the general run of improvements. Since there has been general quality improvement in most goods since the end of the war (especially if we remember that the introduction of new goods must be counted here), it is by no means obvious that such improvements have been greater in our appliances than elsewhere. Indeed, an examination of the opinions of the consumer research organizations tends to show that quality improvements have proceeded at about the normal rate in most of our appliances—there has been only steady, not striking improvement in white goods in this period. To the extent that the effects of such improvement can be characterized by an exponential trend, they will fall in the constant term of our regressions.

One test of the above was made. Improvements seem to have been most striking in electric washing machines, where the automatic or semi-automatic machine has gained ascendancy over the earlier wringer type. These machines have progressed from a very spotty breakdown and repair record to a much higher degree of reliability. As a measure of this improvement we took the ratio of automatic and semi-automatic machines sold to all machines sold nationally and included its logarithm in our regressions. In all cases, this variable had a negative sign and its inclusion only worsened the results. While this result may be due to the special characteristics of the variable used, it does tend to reinforce our judgment about the advisability of treating quality changes only implicitly.

Finally, before leaving this discussion of the model, a few cautionary words are in order. The disease model as just formulated is best suited for the analysis of the growth of stocks of appliances that are not very near saturation. We have made no provision for the fact that the disease cannot spread very fast in percentage terms when nearly everybody has got it. On the other hand, except for refrigerators in the North and East, none of the goods here discussed are approaching saturation so rapidly as to make this an important consideration, although we shall return to it below when discussing the growth of electrification. In general, where it is important, economic variables will be very unimportant, and the variables relating to the size of the susceptible population—H_t, F_t, and M_t—will predominate. It is instructive to look at the geographic pattern of results for refrigerators below with this in mind.

The final equation that we fit (with some or all variables included) is thus (again letting primes stand for natural logarithms):

$$(3.1.6) \quad W'_{it} - W'_{it-1} = A_i + \eta_{i1}(Y_t^{E\prime} - Y_{t-1}^{E\prime}) + \eta_{i2}Y'_t$$

$$+ \eta_{i3}E'_{it} + (\eta_{i4}G'_{it}) + \eta_{i5}(H'_t - H'_{t-1}) + \eta_{i6}(F'_t - F'_{t-1})$$

$$+ \eta_{i7}M'_t + \eta_{i8}P_t^{E\prime} + \eta_{i9}\gamma'_{it} + (\eta_{i10}V_t^{E\prime}) + U_{it}$$

where U_{it} is a random error term with the usual properties assumed.

2. The Data and the Estimating Procedures

The data on W_{it} have been described in the last chapter. It remains to describe the data on the various independent variables.

Y_t and Y_t^E: Y_t is the same as in Chapter 1 and the data thereon are taken from the same sources. Y_t^E was computed from Y_t, using the weights given by Friedman.[10] Friedman's construction and ours differ in one respect, however. He treats the actual incomes of the war years, 1942–45, as irrelevant for the computation of later permanent incomes (since they obviously contained large transitory components). He thus substitutes for them permanent income in 1941 plus two per cent per year to allow for growth. We, on the other hand, do not perform such substitution, believing that the liquid assets which accumulated during the war out of actual incomes played a significant part in financing the meeting of deferred demand for consumer durables.[11]

E_{it}: Except for dryers and water heaters, the Bureau of Labor Statistics Wholesale Price Index gives price indices for our appliances from 1947 to 1957. The electric water heater price index begins in 1950, and the electric dryer index in 1958. We use these indices for all goods save dryers where we use average retail value of dryers sold, computed from value and sales figures in *Electrical Merchandising*. All prices are deflated by the consumer price index. Where an index was given for more than one type of the appliance (ironers, water heaters), we computed a general index by averaging, using the weights given by the Bureau.[12] The sole exception to this was the case of washers, where data from *Electrical Merchandising* on the number of automatic and conventional washers sold nationally permitted us to average the two indices involved using respective sales figures as weights for each year.

Now, the use of the above indices requires some explanation. They are not entirely adequate series for our purposes, as they do not reflect retail prices. This defect is especially marked in appliances, where discount houses and a large variety of easy credit terms affect the retail price. Indeed, the latter circumstance may mean that no price series is really adequate, as the availability of various credit plans may be more important than the ultimate price. On the other

---

[10] *Op. cit.*, p. 146.

[11] In any case, the two permanent incomes are highly correlated, so that this choice has relatively little effect on the results.

[12] Revisions in the weights are negligible in their effects here.

hand, the indices used have one great merit—they apply, by and large, to appliances of constant specifications. Thus the average retail value of refrigerators or ranges sold varies with the average size and capacity thereof; our indices do not so vary, and there is quite a difference between the two corresponding series, as a result. Since this sort of quality variation should clearly not be allowed to influence our price variable, we use the Bureau of Labor Statistics' indices, as stated.

G_{it}: For ranges and water heaters, an index of the wholesale price of the gas-using appliance is available for all necessary years from the source just discussed. No such index is available for gas refrigerators or dryers. Furthermore, no price series whatsoever is readily attainable for either good. This is unimportant in the case of refrigerators, where the gas refrigerator is now a relatively unimportant and declining substitute for the electric appliance, but it is more serious in the case of dryers. This omission, together with the difficulties mentioned above concerning the data on the price of electric dryers, renders our results for dryers almost certainly meaningless.

H_t: The total of residential and rural electric customers listed in the annual *Statistical Bulletin* of the Edison Electric Institute was divided by the population figures described below.

F_t: Population figures were taken from *Personal Income by States since 1929* up to 1953 and from its supplemental article in the *Survey of Current Business* for later years.[13]

M_t: Data on the number of marriages by states were taken from the *Statistical Abstract of the United States*.[14]

P_t^E: This variable was computed as a three-year moving average of residential electricity prices (as described in Chapter 1), save that

---

[13] See Chapter 1 for exact references. Different sources give different estimates of population by states. We used these particular sources to ensure consistency with the estimates of per capita income employed.

[14] The data are sometimes on the number of marriages and sometimes on the number of marriage licenses issued. For Massachusetts in 1953 the *Statistical Abstract* gives no figure. We took our estimate in this case from Commonwealth of Massachusetts, Office of the Secretary, *Annual Report on the Vital Statistics of Massachusetts*, 1953, Table 44.

for 1947 a two-year, and for 1946 a one-year average was taken to exclude the war years from the formation of expectations about postwar real electricity prices.

V_t^E: This variable was computed in the same way as P_t^E from data on the average price of gas per therm computed from sales and revenue data.[15]

γ_{it}: Data on the average kilowatt hour consumption of each appliance per month of average use were taken from the *General Electric Diary*, interpolating or extrapolating where necessary. Figures for washers were computed as weighted averages of the figures for conventional and automatic washers, the weights being the number of washers of each type sold nationally. These data are probably not very accurate. They are the only ones available, however.[16]

This completes our discussion of data sources. One other problem of data remains to be discussed before turning to the estimating procedures used. In every case, save that of water heaters, the period covered is 1946–57 (for water heaters it is 1950–57). This period, however, includes the Korean War. This is important, because the invasion of South Korea and the sending of United States troops that followed led to a wave of durable purchases, as the public feared that such goods would be in short supply as during World War II. This wave was pretty well over by the beginning of 1951, as it became increasingly obvious that such fears were unjustified. However, it is clear that the net change in stocks of appliances during 1950 is a special case and should be excluded from our data. The only other choice would be to introduce a dummy variable which would have the value of unity in 1950 and of zero at all other times. This would be to say that the effects of all other variables on durable purchases remained unchanged during 1950 and that the Korean War simply added to the

---

[15] Data (on all forms of gas combined) from American Gas Association, Bureau of Statistics, *Historical Statistics of the Gas Industry*, New York, 1956; and American Gas Association, *Gas Facts* (annual).

[16] The Edison Electric Institute collects similar data at roughly two-year intervals from estimates made by utility companies. However, these figures are for the existing stock of appliances, not for the increment thereto as required for our purposes.

number of people purchasing durables without influencing such effects. This seems a poor assumption. Rather we should suppose that the Korean War acted by heightening the effects of all other variables, so that a man whose income was not quite high enough, for instance, to make him buy a given appliance ordinarily, made the purchase anyway in the expectation of not being able to do so later on. We thus drop 1950 from our data, but retain 1951 and later years on the assumption that the effects of the Korean War acted in such years only through their effects on the stocks of appliances at the end of 1950.[17]

We turn now to the procedures used in estimating (3.1.6). The large number of variables in that equation makes it impossible to fit it to the data for single states. We have thus to select some method of pooling state data. Clearly, we wish to choose our pools so that there is some assurance of homogeneity in the demand functions for the individual states within each pool

Now, one obvious set of groups of states is already at hand—the groups of Chapter 1, which covariance analysis has already shown to be homogeneous as regards short-run demand and which, further, make demographic sense. However, we might well ask why these groups should be chosen. What has homogeneity with respect to the short-run demand function for electricity got to do with homogeneity in the demand functions for seven particular appliances? It is true that there is no logically necessary connection between the two, yet such a connection seems plausible. Let us inquire as to the reason for this.

Homogeneity of a group of states with respect to the constant term

---

[17] This assumption may not be quite justified. The effect of the Korean War may have been to use up the immediately susceptible population, so to speak, and thus to lower the demonstration effect in later years. On the other hand, this is always the case with an increase in stocks. There were more appliances owned in later years to produce the demonstration effect — more people in common contact with appliance owners. It is thus not obvious that our assumption is wrong. On the whole, it seems better to retain the data for the later years but to discard the observations for 1950.

of the short-run regression equation means that the so far unexplained rates of growth of electricity demand in those states are roughly the same. Considering the major source of such growth, this in turn implies that the rates of growth of the total white good stock (measured in the units of Chapter 1) are roughly the same. Furthermore, we saw clearly in Chapter 1 that different *compositions* of the white good stock were likely to lead to differences in observed short-run price and income elasticities. Homogeneity with respect to these latter parameters, therefore, gives strong presumption to the conclusion that the compositions of the white good stock in the various states in each group are roughly the same. Now, it is perfectly true that homogeneity of white good stock composition and growth rate can come about in other ways than through homogeneity of (3.1.6) for all appliances and similar time paths of the explanatory variables therein. The effects of very different parameters in (3.1.6) for a particular appliance might easily be cancelled out by different growth paths for the explanatory variables. Further, there might be considerable inhomogeneity in (3.1.6) for each appliance and yet homogeneity in the overall composition of the stock of white goods so far as our short-run results are concerned. Yet, if we recall that the groups of Chapter 1 are not wholly arbitrary, but have some *a priori* plausibility from a demographic and topological point of view, it seems rather plausible that such groups should be homogeneous for our purposes.

Even so, we choose to be more cautious and to use groups based on those of Chapter 1 but not identical with them. Here the choice is somewhat arbitrary; the guiding principle is the deletion of those states that do not obviously belong with the major part of the group in every sense (or the splitting of the group, where possible, into two supposed equally homogeneous portions). The groups are as follows (the letters deliberately showing the affinity with the groups of Chapter 1): Group a_1: Massachusetts, Connecticut, Rhode Island; Group a_2: New Jersey, New York; Group b: Pennsylvania, Ohio, Indiana, Michigan, Wisconsin, Missouri; Group c: Minnesota, Iowa, North Dakota, South Dakota, Nebraska, Kansas: Group d: Virginia, North and South Carolina, Georgia, Tennessee, Alabama, Mississippi, Arkansas;

Group e: Louisiana, Texas, New Mexico, Arizona, Nevada; Group f_1: Montana, Idaho, Wyoming, Utah; and Group f_2: Washington, Oregon. Again, there is no guarantee of within-group homogeneity; we must assume this and hope for the best.

One more thing can be done towards securing such homogeneity, however. It is conceivable that our appliance disease has different degrees of infectiousness, so to speak, in different states—that the demonstration effect is naturally stronger in some states than in others. Indeed, if we are wrong in assuming that the demonstration effect is constant, given the values of our explanatory variables, so that the strength of the effect (in percentage terms) is a function of initial stocks (*i.e.*, if the geometric rate of growth of the stock of a particular appliance grows or declines as that growth proceeds), this will be the case. States with higher initial stocks will exhibit a higher constant term in (3.1.6) than do those with lower ones. More generally, if important variables which are approximately constant over time but which vary over states have been left out of our analysis, states might be homogeneous with respect to all slope parameters in (3.1.6), but not with respect to the constant term thereof. Fortunately, this sort of inhomogeneity is easy to eliminate. As in some of the pooled regressions of Chapter 1, we suppress differences in constant terms (and the constant term itself) by measuring all (logarithms of) variables as deviations from their means.

3. The Results

Before proceeding to the results, let us pause to reflect on the large number of approximations, assumptions, and possible errors that they reflect. These fall into three main groups: the model, the data, and the estimating procedures. We shall not go into the number of assumptions involved in our model. Clearly, we suppose them to be better than any alternative feasible set, or we should not use them. Indeed, experimentation shows that the results below, mixed as they are, are superior to those obtained with other formulations and the same data. Nevertheless, it is clear that there are other models which we have not tried—or perhaps, even considered trying—that might do better.

Similarly, we need not further discuss the assumptions underlying our pooling of states, as these have been adequately covered at the end of the last section. It is clear, however, that we can have only moderate assurance that homogeneity has been preserved here.

Finally, it is worth reiterating how poor our data really are; this is the most important point of all. Our estimates of stocks of appliances by states rest not only on the procedures discussed in the last chapter—indeed, we would be content were this the case—they rest fundamentally on the data provided by *Electrical Merchandising*, especially on the data given in that source on sales and stocks by states. *We have no way of evaluating these data; they are the only ones available.* The estimates of state stocks, in particular, are of doubtful quality; they are derived from somewhat spotty reporting in operating utility company surveys and estimates. [18] No results can be better than the data on which they are based, and perhaps it is surprising that our results are as good as they are (it is reassuring to note that our results are better for those appliances where obviously better data are available). *It cannot be pretended, however, that these results are comparable to those of Chapter 1, or that the inferences which we shall draw from them are of comparable reliability.* However, once more, it is the over-all pattern of the results that counts, not the results in any one particular case. This is even more true here than in Chapter 1, since the quality of the data means that the results of any one particular case are not really reliable. The whole impression from the results may be better than the sum of its parts and our conclusions more valid than the measurements on which they rest.

---

[18] Moreover, our model may tend to exaggerate such poor quality, as percentage net changes in our state stock estimates may be largely a compounding of random errors in their levels. On the other hand, such changes are largely made up of sales of new appliances so that our estimates of changes may be a little better than our estimates of the stock levels, if the sales data are good.

TABLE 3.3.1 HOUSEHOLD LONG-RUN REGRESSIONS BY GROUPS OF STATES: WASHING MACHINES, 1946–49, 1951–57

Group	η	Regression Coefficient	Standard Error	R^2	Degrees of Freedom
a₁					
	1	—0.1840	(0.4381)		
	2	+0.0721	(0.1181)		
	3	—0.0257	(0.2224)		
	4	—	—		
	5	—	—		
	6	+0.0311	(0.3155)		
	7	+0.0806	(0.0608)		
	8	—	—		
	9	—	—		
	10	—	—	.5146[aa]	22
a₂					
	1	+0.2791	(0.6422)		
	2	+0.0102	(0.1417)		
	3	+0.2008	(0.2852)		
	4	—	—		
	5	—	—		
	6	+0.3388	(0.6062)		
	7	+0.1042	(0.1205)		
	8	—	—		
	9	—	—		
	10	—	—	.5216[a]	13
b					
	1	+0.7810[a]	(0.3059)		
	2	+0.4705[aaa]	(0.0941)		
	3	—0.3181[a]	(0.1307)		
	4	—	—		
	5	+0.5182	(0.2734)		
	6	+0.3722	(0.3920)		
	7	+0.1196[aaa]	(0.0266)		
	8	—	—		
	9	—	—		
	10	—	—	.6984[aaa]	48
c					
	1	+0.4454	(0.3008)		
	2	+0.1183	(0.0913)		
	3	+0.1670	(0.1285)		

[a] Significant at five per cent level.
[aa] Significant at one per cent level.
[aaa] Significant at one-tenth of one per cent level.

TABLE 3.3.1 HOUSEHOLD LONG-RUN REGRESSIONS BY GROUPS OF STATES: WASHING MACHINES, 1946–49, 1951–57 *(continued)*

Group	η	Regression Coefficient	Standard Error	R^2	Degrees of Freedom
	4	—	—		
	5	+0.4617[aa]	(0.1210)		
	6	+0.2269	(0.3601)		
	7	+0.0723[aa]	(0.0285)		
	8	—	—		
	9	—	—		
	10	—	—	.6379[aaa]	48
d					
	1	+0.0634	(0.4835)		
	2	—0.0439	(0.1307)		
	3	+0.3420	(0.2145)		
	4	—	—		
	5	+0.7992[aaa]	(0.1355)		
	6	+0.1051	(0.3739)		
	7	—	—		
	8	—	—		
	9	—	—		
	10	—	—	.6989[aaa]	58
e					
	1	—0.0565	(0.4377)		
	2	+0.0177	(0.1329)		
	3	+0.0396	(0.1685)		
	4	—	—		
	5	+0.2420[a]	(0.0920)		
	6	+0.1706	(0.2160)		
	7	+0.0329[a]	(0.0155)		
	8	—	—		
	9	—	—		
	10	—	—	.4029[aa]	39
f_1					
	1	+0.1328	(0.3521)		
	2	+0.1048	(0.1391)		
	3	+0.3466[a]	(0.1347)		
	4	—	—		
	5	+0.1535	(0.1981)		

[a] Significant at five per cent level.
[aa] Significant at one per cent level.
[aaa] Significant at one-tenth of one per cent level.

TABLE 3.3.1 HOUSEHOLD LONG-RUN REGRESSIONS BY GROUPS OF STATES: WASHING MACHINES, 1946–49, 1951–57 *(continued)*

Group	η	Regression Coefficient	Standard Error	R^2	Degrees of Freedom
	6	+0.4350[a]	(0.1903)		
	7	—	—		
	8	—	—		
	9	—	—		
	10	—	—	.6590[aaa]	31
f_2					
	1	−1.0136	(1.0174)		
	2	−0.0757	(0.3160)		
	3	+0.1247	(0.2722)		
	4	—	—		
	5	+0.5666	(0.3633)		
	6	+1.1303[a]	(0.5498)		
	7	—	—		
	8	—	—		
	9	—	—		
	10	—	—	.6186[aaa]	22

[a] Significant at five per cent level.
[aaa] Significant at one-tenth of one per cent level.

So much for apologetics. Table 3.3.1 presents the results for washers. We have, in each case, chosen the one or two equations which seem to us best to represent the results. (Because of the large number of variables involved, the tables in this chapter are not in the same form as similar tables elsewhere in this work.)[19]

---

[19] For convenience, we here list the parameters of (3.1.6) together with the variables to which they apply:

η_1: Change in long-run income
η_2: Current income
η_3: Price of appliance
η_4: Price of gas-using substitute
η_5: Change in number of wired households per capita
η_6: Change in population
η_7: Marriages
η_8: Price of electricity
η_9: Kilowatt hours of electricity consumed per time unit of normal use of one physical unit of appliance
η_{10}: Price of gas

We observe the following. First, our model does best in Groups b and c, the fairly urban and the rural states of the Middle West. We do worst in Groups d and e, the South and Southwest, respectively. Since the quality of explanation achieved is high in Groups b and c, this may be some evidence that Groups d and e are inhomogeneous with respect to the demand for washers.

More substantively, nowhere do we find evidence of price-elastic demand. Our price coefficients (η_3) are invariably greater than -1 and almost never significantly negative. Further, the price of electricity has been omitted from the equation for a good reason. Including it here *invariably* gave rise to a corresponding coefficient with positive (*i.e.*, wrong) sign and a general worsening of the results. Similar remarks apply to γ_{it}. So far as these results are concerned, therefore, there is no evidence that the cost of running a new washing machine has any influence on the demand therefor.

Finally, here and later, the change in the number of wired households per capita has been omitted from the equation in the case of Groups a_1 and a_2, as in these areas such change was almost entirely zero or negligible.

We shall have more to say after looking at the results for the other appliances. We turn now to those for refrigerators, shown in Table 3.3.2.

As we should expect, economic variables are unimportant in Groups a_1, a_2, and b, where refrigerators are very near saturation. In fact, they are nearly all unimportant in Group c, as well. Indeed, if economic variables are added to the equation for these groups, they do very badly—but the degree of badness, so to speak, is of interest. In that case, η_1, the coefficient of the change in long-run income, is negative in the first three groups; however, it is far closer to zero in Group b than in the first two groups, and, as seen above, slightly positive for Group c. This progression corresponds to lower saturation in later groups. It is thus highly interesting to note that economic variables are important in the equation for the remaining groups, particularly for the South, Group d. However, there remains the over-all impression that the most important variables are demographic.

TABLE 3.3.2 HOUSEHOLD LONG-RUN REGRESSIONS BY GROUPS OF STATES : REFRIGERATORS, 1946–49, 1951–57

Group	η	Regression Coefficient	Standard Error	R^2	Degrees of Freedom
a_1					
	1	—	—		
	2	—	—		
	3	—	—		
	4	—	—		
	5	—	—		
	6	+0.7066	(0.4910)		
	7	+0.3281[aaa]	(0.0521)		
	8	—	—		
	9	—	—		
	10	—	—	.6149[aaa]	25
a_2					
	1	—	—		
	2	—	—		
	3	—	—		
	4	—	—		
	5	—	—		
	6	+1.0767	(0.5895)		
	7	—	—		
	8	—	—		
	9	—	—		
	10	—	—	.1640	17
b					
	1	—	—		
	2	—	—		
	3	—	—		
	4	—	—		
	5	+0.8592[aa]	(0.3152)		
	6	+0.8877	(0.5282)		
	7	+0.0779[a]	(0.0358)		
	8	—	—		
	9	—	—		
	10	—	—	.2495[aa]	51
c					
	1	+0.2972	(0.1811)		
	2	—	—		

[a] Significant at five per cent level.
[aa] Significant at one per cent level.
[aaa] Significant at one-tenth of one per cent level.

TABLE 3.3.2 HOUSEHOLD LONG-RUN REGRESSIONS BY GROUPS OF STATES: REFRIGERATORS, 1946–49, 1951–57 *(continued)*

Group	η	Regression Coefficient	Standard Error	R^2	Degrees of Freedom
	3	—	—		
	4	—	—		
	5	+1.3188[aaa]	(0.1103)		
	6	+1.4835[aa]	(0.4401)		
	7	+0.0167	(0.0308)		
	8	—	—		
	9	—	—		
	10	—	—	.7463[aaa]	50
d Equation I:					
	1	+0.3494	(0.7718)		
	2	+0.4079	(0.2182)		
	3	—0.0993	(0.1679)		
	4	—	—		
	5	+0.5642[aaa]	(0.1520)		
	6	+0.9572[a]	(0.3813)		
	7	—	—		
	8	—	—		
	9	—	—		
	10	—	—	.6436[aaa]	58
d Equation II:					
	1	+0.1582	(0.6809)		
	2	+0.5290[a]	(0.2125)		
	3	+0.0716	(0.1721)		
	4	—	—		
	5	+0.8019[aaa]	(0.1699)		
	6	+1.3703[aaa]	(0.3945)		
	7	—	—		
	8	—0.2331[aa]	(0.0874)		
	9	—	—		
	10	—	—	.6830[aaa]	57
e					
	1	+0.9375	(0.9173)		
	2	+0.4684	(0.2927)		
	3	—0.0305	(0.2163)		
	4	—	—		
	5	+0.2926	(0.1814)		

[a] Significant at five per cent level.
[aa] Significant at one per cent level.
[aaa] Significant at one-tenth of one per cent level.

TABLE 3.3.2 HOUSEHOLD LONG-RUN REGRESSIONS BY GROUPS OF STATES: REFRIGERATORS, 1946–49, 1951–57 *(continued)*

Group	η	Regression Coefficient	Standard Error	R^2	Degrees of Freedom
	6	+0.8689[a]	(0.4128)		
	7	+0.0270	(0.0469)		
	8	—	—		
	9	—	—		
	10	—	—	.4345[aaa]	39
f_1 Equation I:					
	1	—	—		
	2	+0.2488[a]	(0.0990)		
	3	+0.1626	(0.0830)		
	4	—	—		
	5	+0.5260[a]	(0.2350)		
	6	+1.0502[aa]	(0.2931)		
	7	—	—		
	8	—	—		
	9	—	—		
	10	—	—	.6806[aaa]	32
f_1 Equation II:					
	1	+0.1556	(0.6045)		
	2	+0.3030	(0.2331)		
	3	+0.1428	(0.0978)		
	4	—	—		
	5	+0.5286[a]	(0.2387)		
	6	+1.0644[aa]	(0.3026)		
	7	—	—		
	8	—	—		
	9	—	—		
	10	—	—	.6812[aaa]	31
f_2					
	1	—	—		
	2	+0.5551	(0.2836)		
	3	+0.0742	(0.1594)		
	4	—	—		
	5	+1.0133[a]	(0.3926)		
	6	+1.3391	(0.7352)		
	7	—	—		
	8	—	—		
	9	—	—		
	10	—	—	.7150[aaa]	14

[a] Significant at five per cent level.
[aa] Significant at one per cent level.
[aaa] Significant at one-tenth of one per cent level.

Turning now to the coefficients of the economic variables, where they appear, we observe that the change in long-run income never seems to be too important. By and large, it is current income that matters, if anything does. This is sensible; the threshold income for refrigerators must be very low, as a refrigerator is considered a necessity. What matters, therefore, is not so much the long-run position as the ability to expend current income on a down payment.

Next, we observe that again the price of the appliance is unimportant. This is even more marked here than in the case of washers, as we should expect. We shall hypothesize concerning this below.

Finally, there is some evidence for the effect of the price of electricity in the South. This may be due to the existence of a relatively larger stock of old gas-using refrigerators in that area, or to special circumstances connected with the Tennessee Valley Authority. There is no evidence for such an effect in other regions.

The results for ironers are presented in Table 3.3.3. Here, for the first time, we find evidence of substantial elasticity with respect to appliance price. There are coefficients algebraically less than minus one in two groups and the general impression is one of greater price sensitivity than in the case of the first two white goods discussed.

There is also considerable sensitivity to changes in long-run income in some regions, but not in others, although in the latter there is considerable sensitivity to current income. As a very tentative hypothesis, we offer the explanation that people, particularly in poorer areas, worry more about meeting the down payment on an appliance than about the eventual full cost thereof. We shall return to this below.

As before, there is no evidence that the cost of operating an ironer has any effect on demand.

Table 3.3.4 presents the results for electric ranges. These results are not even as good as those just presented, and some discussion is in order before viewing them. Unlike the three goods analyzed above, electric ranges are subject to very strong competition from a gas-using substitute. Indeed, gas ranges are a much larger part of the total stock of ranges than are electric ranges. This has several consequences. Aside from the including of the price of gas ranges and the price of gas

TABLE 3.3.3 HOUSEHOLD LONG-RUN REGRESSIONS BY GROUPS OF STATES: IRONING MACHINES, 1946–49, 1951–57

Group	η	Regression Coefficient	Standard Error	R^2	Degrees of Freedom
a_1					
	1	+0.6491	(1.5054)		
	2	+0.4312	(0.3298)		
	3	−1.0417	(0.8981)		
	4	—	—		
	5	—	—		
	6	+0.8338	(1.0748)		
	7	+0.3642[aa]	(0.1285)		
	8	—	—		
	9	—	—		
	10	—	—	.6237[aaa]	22
a_2					
	1	+1.2291	(0.5839)		
	2	+0.4040[aa]	(0.1230)		
	3	+0.2248	(0.3327)		
	4	—	—		
	5	—	—		
	6	+1.0290	(0.5631)		
	7	+0.3176[aa]	(0.0886)		
	8	—	—		
	9	—	—		
	10	—	—	.8845[aaa]	13
b					
	1	+1.4940[aaa]	(0.3627)		
	2	+0.6873[aaa]	(0.0921)		
	3	−0.3277	(0.2464)		
	4	—	—		
	5	+0.2911	(0.3390)		
	6	+0.3674	(0.4968)		
	7	+0.1144[aaa]	(0.0303)		
	8	—	—		
	9	—	—		
	10	—	—	.8179[aaa]	48
c					
	1	+1.4292[aa]	(0.4459)		
	2	+0.3900	(0.1339)		
	3	−0.5177	(0.3618)		
	4	—	—		
	5	+1.4904[aaa]	(0.1496)		

[aa] Significant at one per cent level.
[aaa] Significant at one-tenth of one per cent level.

TABLE 3.3.3 HOUSEHOLD LONG-RUN REGRESSIONS BY GROUPS OF STATES: IRONING MACHINES, 1946–49, 1951–57 *(continued)*

Group	η	Regression Coefficient	Standard Error	R^2	Degrees of Freedom
	6	$+0.5536$	(0.6188)		
	7	$+0.0935$[a]	(0.0446)		
	8	—	—		
	9	—	—		
	10	—	—	.7488[aaa]	48
d					
	1	—	—		
	2	$+0.4012$[aa]	(0.1264)		
	3	-1.5177[aa]	(0.4923)		
	4	—	—		
	5	$+1.6359$[aaa]	(0.2073)		
	6	$+2.1092$[aa]	(0.5859)		
	7	—	—		
	8	—	—		
	9	—	—		
	10	—	—	.8201[aaa]	59
	1	—	—		
e					
	2	$+0.6040$[aaa]	(0.1121)		
	3	-0.7750	(0.6575)		
	4	—	—		
	5	$+0.5428$[a]	(0.2414)		
	6	$+0.6860$[aaa]	(0.0763)		
	7	—	—		
	8	—	—		
	9	—	—		
	10	—	—	.7936[aaa]	41
f_1					
	1	$+1.4060$	(0.9606)		
	2	$+0.8996$[a]	(0.3571)		
	3	-0.2230	(0.5522)		
	4	—	—		
	5	$+0.5674$	(0.3799)		
	6	$+1.1733$[a]	(0.5389)		
	7	—	—		
	8	—	—		
	9	—	—		
	10	—	—	.4628[aaa]	31

[a] Significant at five per cent level.
[aa] Significant at one per cent level.
[aaa] Significant at one-tenth of one per cent level.

TABLE 3.3.3 HOUSEHOLD LONG-RUN REGRESSIONS BY GROUPS OF STATES: IRONING MACHINES, 1946–49, 1951–57 *(continued)*

Group	η	Regression Coefficient	Standard Error	R^2	Degrees of Freedom
f_2					
1	—	—			
2	$+0.8522$[a]	(0.3412)			
3	$+0.5714$	(0.8183)			
4	—	—			
5	$+2.1883$[aa]	(0.5756)			
6	$+2.7585$[a]	(1.1310)			
7	—	—			
8	—	—			
9	—	—			
10	—	—		.7027[aaa]	14

[a] Significant at five per cent level.
[aa] Significant at one per cent level.
[aaa] Significant at one-tenth of one per cent level.

explicitly in the analysis, it means that households can decrease their stock of the electric appliances much more easily here than in the case of most other goods. Instead of not replacing the electrical appliance when it ages, they can replace it with the gas-using substitute. This means that there is no necessity for us to find positive coefficients for the demographic variables; increases in the susceptible population may be accompanied by decreases in the stock of electric ranges as potential purchasers (including those ready to replace existing electric ranges) are inoculated against the electric range disease with the gas range vaccine. Furthermore, increases in income—either long-run or current—may also be accompanied by decreases in the stock of electric ranges, other things being equal, as owners of electric ranges use the increased income to replace them with gas ranges. We find occasional, but by no means universal evidence of all these effects; however, such evidence is a little weak, since we should expect it to be accompanied by large elasticities with respect to the price of electric and the price of gas ranges, and this we do not find. Despite the argument, given after the table, concerning such price effects, this is somewhat disturbing.

TABLE 3.3.4 HOUSEHOLD LONG-RUN REGRESSIONS BY GROUPS OF STATES: ELECTRIC RANGES, 1946–49, 1951–57

Group	η	Regression Coefficient	Standard Error	R^2	Degrees of Freedom
a_1 Equation I:					
	1	+2.3413[a]	(0.9517)		
	2	+0.4549	(0.3257)		
	3	+0.2126	(0.3584)		
	4	−0.1317	(0.3079)		
	5	—	—		
	6	−0.0162	(0.6119)		
	7	+0.1804[a]	(0.0789)		
	8	—	—		
	9	—	—		
	10	—	—	.6845[aaa]	21
a_1 Equation II:					
	1	+0.8512	(0.9620)		
	2	+0.0980	(0.2779)		
	3	−0.3988	(0.3169)		
	4	+0.6736[a]	(0.3111)		
	5	—	—		
	6	+0.2971	(0.5083)		
	7	+0.0541	(0.0831)		
	8	+0.2804	(0.1516)		
	9	—	—		
	10	+0.4085[aa]	(0.1292)	.8355[aaa]	19
a_2 Equation I:					
	1	−1.2374	(0.9187)		
	2	−0.0118	(0.3181)		
	3	+0.1370	(0.4294)		
	4	+0.1787	(0.3467)		
	5	—	—		
	6	+0.6388	(1.0257)		
	7	—	—		
	8	—	—		
	9	—	—		
	10	—	—	.6374[aa]	13

[a] Significant at five per cent level.
[aa] Significant at one per cent level.
[aaa] Significant at one-tenth of one per cent level.

TABLE 3.3.4 HOUSEHOLD LONG-RUN REGRESSIONS BY GROUPS OF STATES: ELECTRIC RANGES, 1946–49, 1951–57 *(continued)*

Group	η	Regression Coefficient	Standard Error	R^2	Degrees of Freedom
a₂ Equation II:					
	1	−1.0568	(1.1039)		
	2	−0.4245	(0.5964)		
	3	−0.1508	(0.4185)		
	4	+0.4465	(0.3670)		
	5	—	—		
	6	+0.9338	(0.9504)		
	7	—	—		
	8	+0.0137	(0.3316)		
	9	—	—		
	10	+0.4377	(0.4150)	.8121ᵃᵃᵃ	11
b Equation I:					
	1	+0.1803	(0.7508)		
	2	+0.1251	(0.2917)		
	3	+0.1364	(0.2973)		
	4	−0.2665	(0.2225)		
	5	+0.6662	(0.5231)		
	6	+0.7518	(0.7056)		
	7	+0.1217ᵃᵃ	(0.0429)		
	8	—	—		
	9	—	—		
	10	—	—	.6184ᵃᵃᵃ	47
b Equation II:					
	1	+0.3968	(0.6911)		
	2	+0.1954	(0.2889)		
	3	−0.3389	(0.2990)		
	4	+0.1070	(0.2157)		
	5	+0.0447	(0.4976)		
	6	+0.0134	(0.6496)		
	7	+0.0726	(0.0398)		
	8	+0.2974ᵃᵃ	(0.1080)		
	9	—	—		
	10	+0.0536	(0.0708)	.7205ᵃᵃᵃ	45
c Equation I:					
	1	+0.8113	(0.5730)		
	2	+0.1648	(0.1807)		
	3	+0.6034ᵃᵃ	(0.2314)		

ᵃᵃ Significant at one per cent level.
ᵃᵃᵃ Significant at one-tenth of one per cent level.

TABLE 3.3.4 HOUSEHOLD LONG-RUN REGRESSIONS BY GROUPS OF STATES: ELECTRIC RANGES, 1946–49, 1951–57 *(continued)*

Group	η	Regression Coefficient	Standard Error	R^2	Degrees of Freedom
	4	—0.0246	(0.2147)		
	5	+0.6746[a]	(0.2804)		
	6	—0.0417	(0.5242)		
	7	—	—		
	8	—	—		
	9	—	—		
	10	—	—	.6410[aaa]	48
c Equation II:					
	1	+0.1155	(0.5326)		
	2	—0.0185	(0.1711)		
	3	—0.1881	(0.2580)		
	4	+0.3540	(0.2113)		
	5	+0.7908[aa]	(0.2407)		
	6	+0.2204	(0.6925)		
	7	—	—		
	8	+0.4026[aa]	(0.1303)		
	9	—	—		
	10	+0.1073	(0.0782)	.7495[aaa]	46
d Equation I:					
	1	+0.2747	(0.4649)		
	2	+0.1418	(0.1858)		
	3	+0.1437	(0.2177)		
	4	—0.1832	(0.1960)		
	5	+0.7209[aaa]	(0.1446)		
	6	+1.1871[aaa]	(0.2992)		
	7	+0.0170	(0.0140)		
	8	—	—		
	9	—	—		
	10	—	—	.8583[aaa]	56
d Equation II:					
	1	+0.2845	(0.4656)		
	2	+0.0951	(0.1917)		
	3	+0.0800	(0.2419)		
	4	—0.0970	(0.2070)		
	5	+0.6729[aaa]	(0.1484)		

[a] Significant at five per cent level.
[aa] Significant at one per cent level.
[aaa] Significant at one-tenth of one per cent level.

TABLE 3.3.4 HOUSEHOLD LONG-RUN REGRESSIONS BY GROUPS OF STATES: ELECTRIC RANGES, 1946–49, 1951–57   *(continued)*

Group	η	Regression Coefficient	Standard Error	R^2	Degrees of Freedom
	6	+ 1.0660[aaa]	(0.3136)		
	7	+ 0.0172	(0.0140)		
	8	+ 0.1031	(0.0714)		
	9	—	—		
	10	— 0.0337	(0.0449)	.8636[aaa]	54
e Equation I:					
	1	— 1.1669	(0.8743)		
	2	— 0.0417	(0.3190)		
	3	+ 0.3153	(0.2884)		
	4	— 0.0280	(0.2741)		
	5	+ 0.0658	(0.1577)		
	6	+ 0.3110	(0.3593)		
	7	+ 0.0074	(0.0385)		
	8	—	—		
	9	—	—		
	10	—	—	.4208[aaa]	38
e Equation II:					
	1	+ 0.3079	(0.8449)		
	2	+ 0.5518	(0.3076)		
	3	— 0.0250	(0.2806)		
	4	+ 0.1600	(0.2685)		
	5	+ 0.0139	(0.1350)		
	6	+ 0.1816	(0.3074)		
	7	+ 0.0290	(0.0335)		
	8	— 0.1368	(0.0697)		
	9	—	—		
	10	+ 0.3033[aaa]	(0.0758)	.6042[aaa]	36
f₁ Equation I:					
	1	— 0.3561	(1.0928)		
	2	— 0.2215	(0.4683)		
	3	+ 0.5256	(0.3523)		
	4	— 0.3878	(0.2788)		
	5	+ 0.0782	(0.4875)		
	6	+ 0.2750	(0.5926)		
	7	—	—		

[aaa] Significant at one-tenth of one per cent level.

TABLE 3.3.4 HOUSEHOLD LONG-RUN REGRESSIONS BY GROUPS OF STATES: ELECTRIC RANGES, 1946–49, 1951–57 *(continued)*

Group	η	Regression Coefficient	Standard Error	R^2	Degrees of Freedom
	8	—	—		
	9	—	—		
	10	—	—	.4733[aaa]	30
f_1 Equation II:					
	1	+0.1080	(1.4863)		
	2	—0.0312	(0.6159)		
	3	+0.2496	(0.4129)		
	4	—0.2018	(0.3196)		
	5	—0.4725	(0.6652)		
	6	—0.1188	(0.6715)		
	7	—	—		
	8	+0.1800	(0.1854)		
	9	—	—		
	10	+0.0216	(0.0376)	.5035[aaa]	28
f_2 Equation I:					
	1	—1.0492	(0.9485)		
	2	—0.2258	(0.3208)		
	3	+0.0706	(0.2261)		
	4	—0.3456	(0.1752)		
	5	+0.9042[a]	(0.3213)		
	6	+1.7195[a]	(0.5394)		
	7	+0.1448[a]	(0.0519)		
	8	—	—		
	9	—	—		
	10	—	—	.9280[aaa]	11
f_2 Equation II:					
	1	—1.2677	(1.4042)		
	2	—0.3785	(0.4023)		
	3	—0.1668	(0.2713)		
	4	—0.1608	(0.2487)		
	5	+0.4441	(0.4331)		
	6	+1.5285[a]	(0.5439)		
	7	+0.1517[a]	(0.0568)		
	8	+0.1708	(0.1424)		
	9	—	—		
	10	+0.1179	(0.1470)	.9432[aaa]	9

[a] Significant at five per cent level.
[aaa] Significant at one-tenth of one per cent level.

We have presented two equations for each group. The first of these does not contain the prices of electricity or of gas, the second one does. While the signs on the latter two coefficients are generally not what we should expect *a priori* (negative and positive, respectively), we include them, nonetheless, because such inclusion seems to make a large difference in the other coefficients of the equation—generally in the direction of greater plausibility. This is not strong evidence for the effect of operating costs on demand, but it is some evidence, since the last two coefficients, when they have the wrong sign, are usually small and non-significant.

The results are hardly impressive and suggest inhomogeneity in some of our groups; nevertheless, the introduction of electricity and gas prices does serve to improve them, especially in Group e, the Southwest, where this effect cannot be doubted. Once more we find no large price effects.

Before discussing the general conclusions that may be drawn from the four sets of results just presented, we must briefly remark on the results obtained (but not presented) for freezers, dryers, and water heaters. It will be recalled that our stocks by states estimates for these three goods are far less reliable than those for the first four appliances, and that additional data on dryers, in particular, are missing or of dubious quality. It therefore comes as no surprise to discover that the regression results for these three goods are simply not worth presenting; there is too much noise in the data. One important and outstanding fact does emerge from these results, however. In the regressions for water heaters—as nowhere else in either the results presented or those omitted—the coefficient of the price of electricity has a negative sign and the coefficient of the price of gas a positive sign in almost every group. It is hard to believe that this is an accident; rather, taken together with the reported results, it suggests the following conclusion: for major appliances, at least, the operating costs of an electric white good affect appliance demand solely, if at all, where those costs are high, and where the appliance is subject to substantial gas competition. Thus the only evidence of such an effect in our results is for ranges and water heaters in general, and for refrigerators in the South. Even for these goods, the evidence is not strong, but there is no such evidence as regards the other appliances studied. (Clearly, the very poor quality of the available data makes it difficult to tell whether such an effect exists for dryers where there is an important gas-using substitute; it probably does.) Further, where it exists, the effect seems to be fairly small, though perhaps not entirely negligible.

These remarks naturally lead to a discussion of three further questions. First, we spoke above of the effects of operating cost; yet γ_{it}, the technological component thereof, so to speak, appeared in none of our results. How can this be? The answer is that γ_{it} did not change very much for any of the goods where we find operating costs to have an effect. Changes were slow in refrigerators, and, while there were large changes in the wattage ratings of water heaters and especially of ranges (almost a doubling), this is not the same as a change in γ_{it}. The point is that changes in wattage ratings represent essentially changes in capacity—in the case of ranges, changes in the number of burners or other units available for simultaneous use. They do not represent changes in the amount of power required to perform given functions (although, of course, they may affect this somewhat by providing alternative means of doing the same thing—e.g., of cooking a meal). Thus, for example, γ_{it} for ranges is essentially a technological constant. It is determined by the amount of electric energy necessary to heat certain substances to certain temperatures. Hence our conclusion above can hold for operating costs even though we never find any effects from the γ_{it}.

Second, our conclusion as to the effects of operating costs on the demand for major appliances leads naturally to a consideration of such effects in the case of the demand for minor ones. Here we have no evidence; however, something may still be ventured. On the one hand, operating costs for most minor appliances are relatively low; on the other, there are substitutes available for most of them, although the substitutes may take the form of traditional ways of performing the same functions rather than of appliances with other energy sources. In balance, it is not clear what the answer is. It is probably safe to say that very high operating costs would reduce the demand for those minor appliances where alternative methods of performing the same function are readily available.

Finally, we have the question of consistency. We found in Chapter 1 fairly clear evidence of the effect of electricity price on the intensity of use of the existing appliance stock. Is this inconsistent with a finding that potential operating costs do not appreciably affect the demand for most appliances? Of course not. In the first place, since there is some tendency for the operating-costs effect to operate in the case of appliances whose electricity consumptions (and hence whose operating costs) are greatest, it may be that the price effects of Chapter 1 are accounted for entirely by the effects on the use of such appliances. Secondly, it is quite possible that a household would only consider the costs of running an appliance after it is actually in use. Few people let future operating costs determine whether or not their house will be lit electrically, but many people remember to shut off the lights when not in use because of the money (or perhaps the money-saving habit) involved. Finally, such behavior is by no means irrational, given the indivisibility of individual appliance possessions. Operating costs may continously influence the demand for the services of a given appliance, yet may never rise high enough to reduce that demand to zero either when viewed *ex ante* or, especially, once the cost of the appliance has become a sunk cost.

We turn now to the other issues raised by the results reported above. The first of these is that of the effect (or rather of the non-existence of the effect) of appliance prices. Save in the case of ironers, we found no substantial effect here. To an extent, this is not too surprising; refrigerators are certainly necessities and washers are perhaps becoming so. Further, it is clear that our results for ranges are none too good, so perhaps we ought not to consider this case. Nevertheless, the appearance of such low coefficients seems to require further explanation. Such explanation probably lies in the nature of the price series used and in the way in which appliance purchases are made and financed. Indeed, we have already hinted at it in discussing our price series.

Our price series is one of wholesale prices. While we use it because no comparable series of retail prices is readily obtainable for most goods, it has the defect that it does not adequately reflect the terms on which appliances are bought. Indeed, it is doubtful whether any constructed series of prices could do so, because appliances are sold on a large and bewildering variety of credit plans. It may well be the case that the terms on which an appliance is available—the number and size of monthly payments and, especially, the size of the initial down payment—are far more important in influencing demand than is the total cost of the good. In that case, we should find, as we do, that demand is inelastic with respect to total appliance price. Further, this point should be weakest for appliances which are farthest from being necessities and which are inexpensive relative to other appliances. It is clear that, of the four appliances studied above, this description applies best to ironers, and, accordingly, we observe somewhat greater price effects here.

Furthermore, this hypothesis has implications for the two income variables used. If the terms of appliance purchase have the effect stated, then our model is correct in including changes in long-run income and the level of current income. We interpreted the inclusion of changes in long-run income as representing the number of people crossing a certain minimum threshold of long-run income. Now that threshold can be slightly further interpreted: it is the long-run income level at which people are willing to undertake a certain amount of (additional) debt. However, it is clear that current income must be important too, for the additional debt will only be undertaken when the down payment can be easily afforded and this is more likely when current income is high. Hence we find that both income variables are fairly important. It should further be true that the richer the community the less important (relatively) the current income variable is, especially for goods where total cost is relatively low. As observed above, we find such a tendency in the case of ironers.

We turn now to the demographic variables. First, we observe that there is ample evidence that all three of these are important—a result which is chiefly interesting as regards marriages. Second, concentrating in the change in the number of wired households per capita and change in population, we observe a general (but not a universal) tendency for the second variable to have a greater coefficient than the first. Increases in the number of wired households that come about through increases in population have a greater effect on appliance demand than do increases that come about through more wiring with a given population. This is understandable. Wired households are near saturation in most parts of the country, and certainly, even in the South, more households are wired than not. Increases in the number of wired households with given population therefore tend to involve the addition to the wired population of relatively poor households whose immediate contribution to the demand for appliances is small. Increases in the number of wired households that come about through increases in population, on the other hand, do not have this property. They come about principally through new construction, and the addition of households in this way is likely to be the addition of richer households than in the previous case. There can be no doubt, however, that both variables—both modes of wired household growth—are the most important determinants of appliance demand.

4. The Rate of Electrification

One more subject requires discussion before going on to consider the conclusions that may be drawn from all the foregoing analysis for the total demand (long- and short-run) for electricity by households; the subject in question is that of the determinants of the rate of growth of the number of wired households per capita, of the rate of electrification itself. The reason that consideration of this problem is important is that the rate of growth of wired households per capita appears in our explanation of the rate of growth of the stock of white goods and that it is the one variable which so appears which conceivably might be influenced by the price of electricity. If such influence does exist, we must certainly take account of it in our conclusions concerning the total price elasticity of household electricity demand.

The equation used for purposes of analyzing the growth in question is similar to those used for appliance demand. It is (with all variables present), where primes denote logarithms:

$$(3.4.1) \quad (H'_t - H'_{t-1}) = C' + \pi_1(\mu - H_{t-1})' + \pi_2 H'_{t-1} + \pi_3 Y'_t$$
$$+ \pi_4(Y_t^{E\prime} - Y_{t-1}^{E\prime}) + \pi_5 P_t^{E\prime} + U_t$$

Here, C, the π_i, and μ are constant parameters; U_t is a random disturbance with the usual properties; the variables have already been defined. The equation requires some discussion.

It is principally the appearance of the two terms multiplying π_1 and π_2 that makes this equation differ from those already used. Let us discuss them one at a time. The term multiplying π_1 is designed to represent the fact that the number of wired households per capita cannot grow when all households are wired—more generally, that the closer one gets to such a maximum the slower is the percentage rate of growth likely to be, as fewer households remain to be wired relative to the number already electrified. Accordingly, μ represents the total number of households per capita and is assumed constant over time for each state for want of better information.

As our estimate of μ for each state, we take the reciprocal of the number of persons per household in that state in 1950 as given in the *Statistical Abstract*. This procedure is subject to some minor limitations arising from the existence of an institutional population and the difficulties of measurement of H_t, and, accordingly, it is occasionally necessary to take μ as the actual maximum achieved by H_t plus an amount just large enough to let all logarithms exist (.0001, here). This was not necessary for the states reported below, by and large, since H_t is not very near μ in these.

The inclusion of H'_{t-1} as an explicit explanatory variable is designed to take account of possible acceleration or deceleration in electrification. We do not have figures on the cost of wiring the average household and are obliged to assume it constant. The inclusion of H'_{t-1} may help to overcome this deficiency in the following way. The cost of wiring a given household in a very incompletely electrified state depends to some extent on the size and coverage of the existing

TABLE 3.4.1 HOUSEHOLD LONG-RUN REGRESSIONS: THE RATE OF ELECTRIFICATION IN SOUTHERN STATES, 1946–57

State	π	Regression Coefficient	Standard Error	R^2	Degrees of Freedom
Virginia:					
	1	+0.0244[aa]	(0.0042)		
	2	—	—		
	3	+0.7898[a]	(0.1786)		
	4	+1.2186[a]	(0.3481)		
	5	—0.2517[a]	(0.1049)	.9807[aaa]	6
North and South Carolina:					
	1	+0.0176[a]	(0.0059)		
	2	—	—		
	3	+0.5652	(0.3466)		
	4	+1.1451	(1.0773)		
	5	—	—	.8743[aaa]	7
Georgia:					
	1	+0.0124[a]	(0.0050)		
	2	—	—		
	3	+0.2599[a]	(0.0860)		
	4	—	—		
	5	—	—	.7709[aa]	8
Tennessee:					
	1	+0.0006	(0.0052)		
	2	—	—		
	3	+0.3881[a]	(0.1205)		
	4	—	—		
	5	—	—	.6937[aa]	8
Alabama:					
	1	+0.0109	(0.0063)		
	2	—	—		
	3	+0.2572[a]	(0.1027)		
	4	—	—		
	5	—	—	.6528[a]	8

[a] Significant at five per cent level.
[aa] Significant at one per cent level.
[aaa] Significant at one-tenth of one per cent level.

TABLE 3.4.1   HOUSEHOLD LONG-RUN REGRESSIONS: THE RATE OF ELECTRIFICATION IN SOUTHERN STATES, 1946–57   *(continued)*

State	π	Regression Coefficient	Standard Error	R^2	Degrees of Freedom
Mississippi Equation I:					
	1	+0.0290[aa]	(0.0065)		
	2	—	—		
	3	+0.7026[a]	(0.2284)		
	4	+2.2029	(0.9791)		
	5	—	—	.8521[aa]	7
Mississippi Equation II:					
	1	+0.0355[a]	(0.0126)		
	2	—	—		
	3	+1.0424	(0.6106)		
	4	+3.1484	(1.8701)		
	5	—0.1421	(0.2349)	.8606[aa]	6
Arkansas:					
	1	+0.0211[a]	(0.0080)		
	2	—	—		
	3	+0.3434[a]	(0.1573)		
	4	—	—		
	5	—	—	.6547[a]	8
Louisiana:					
	1	+0.0117[a]	(0.0042)		
	2	—	—		
	3	+0.6590[aa]	(0.1369)		
	4	+1.5926	(0.7078)		
	5	—0.0901[a]	(0.0390)	.9435[aaa]	6

[a] Significant at five per cent level.
[aa] Significant at one per cent level.
[aaa] Significant at one-tenth of one per cent level.

electric grid. In other words, to some extent, the higher H_{t-1}, the lower will be the costs of wiring new households. Hence, to some extent, the inclusion of H'_{t-1} provides a surrogate for a missing cost variable. We should not expect the effect here to be large, however, as the argument just given seems most applicable to the case of very low initial H_t.

For π_1 and π_2 both positive, the inclusion of the two terms just discussed amounts to assuming an S-shaped growth curve, other things being equal, with the relative magnitudes of π_1 and π_2 determining the exact curvature of the S. In other words, other things being equal, the number of wired households per capita is assumed to grow first slowly, then faster and faster, then more slowly again, finally approaching μ as an asymptote.

The other variables in (3.4.1) need no discussion, as they perform the same functions as elsewhere in this chapter. We should not expect the term in long-run income to play much of a role, however, as the income threshold for electrification must be very low.

As might be expected, the application of (3.4.1) to data for 1946–57 yields results of little interest save in the Southern states (we do not have enough data to make a prewar analysis). The results for those states are presented in Table 3.4.1. The constant term is omitted as being of no special interest (it is not independent of units of measurement). As before, more than one equation is presented where interesting.

Results for some other under-electrified states are similar. Nowhere does H_{t-1} play a direct role; current income does better than changes in long-run income; and there is no evidence of a price effect other than that presented; although, of course, this is not to say that such an effect may not have been present in the prewar period when the state of electrification was much lower.

5. Household Electricity Demand: Conclusions

We have reached the end of our empirical investigation of household demand for electricity. We must now consider some of the implications of the results obtained.

It is clear from the original demand function fitted (1.1.13), that the price (or income) elasticity of household electricity demand is the sum of two elasticities: one, which we have called the "short-run" elasticity, being the elasticity of the intensity of use of the existing white good stock, and the other, which we have called the "long-run" elasticity, being the elasticity of demand for the white goods stock itself. To put it slightly differently, the effects of an electricity price change which is maintained for some time consist of effects on the size of the appliance stock plus effects on the intensity of use thereof.[20] In Chapter 1, we were concerned with the latter effects, and found interesting patterns therein; this chapter has discussed the former effects, and found them to be small, on the whole.

This latter conclusion will be reinforced if we recall that what is at issue here is the effect of the price of electricity on the white good stock as a whole. We found evidence of such an effect only for fairly special cases.

One point must be made, however, and that is that we did tend to find greater evidence of effects of the price of electricity on the white good stock in the South and Southwest than elsewhere. This is not unexpected, since we already know that those states are among those with highest short-run price elasticity. The fact that high short-run price elasticity was found for nearly all states for the prewar period makes us suspect that there may have been long-run price effects as well in that period for all states.

Now, all this, coupled with our conclusions and predictions at the end of Chapter 1, has some bearing on one limited aspect of the experience of the Tennessee Valley Authority. As is well known, during the thirties TVA lowered electricity rates in its area drastically and found electricity demand to be far more elastic than had previously been supposed. Indeed, so dramatic was this experience that the claim was (and to some extent still is) made that electric power companies in general tend to underestimate (absolutely) the price elasticity of demand, and hence to charge needlessly high rates. This is one—but by no means the only—facet of the idea that TVA rates should serve as a "yardstick" for electricity rates elsewhere.

---

[20] The effects involving increased intensity of use of additions to stock are of the second order of smallness and disappear when passing to the limit and evaluating elasticity as a logarithmic derivative.

Now, our results of the next chapter show that this argument may conceivably be correct so far as industrial electricity demand is concerned, but it is clear from our results so far that its application is very limited so far as the demand from households is involved. If our prewar results are correct, the claim that electricity demand was reasonably elastic (at least, more so than had previously been supposed) was quite justified when it was made. Indeed, the fact of the success of the TVA low-price experiment gives us more faith in our prewar results. However, it is clear that that claim would not be justified today for the major part of the country—our Groups A–C. In such areas we find substantially lower (absolute) price elasticity than was the case in the thirties or is the case still in the economically younger states. Furthermore, our prediction is for decreasing price (and increasing short-run income) elasticity in those parts of the nation which still exhibit considerable price sensitivity. If this is correct, then the lesson of the TVA low price experiment (but not necessarily of other aspects of the TVA experience) is an important one, but one rather limited in both time and space.

One last conclusion is in order here; this one concerning growth. It seems clear from both the growth rates found in our short-run analysis and the differing results for the demand for various white goods— for refrigerators, in particular—as well as from the data of Appendix B, that the high growth rate of electricity demand relative to the economy as a whole has been largely supported by technological change, by the introduction of new goods. As older electric appliances approach saturation, their growth rate tends largely to be determined by the rate of growth of population, of long-run income, perhaps, and of electrification. New appliances, however, tend to grow faster than this and tend to be subject to other influences, such as the level of current income. Perhaps it would be more correct to say that these last remarks are indicated rather than shown by our data and results.

CHAPTER 4

ELECTRICITY DEMAND BY INDUSTRY

1. The Constant Technology Model: Aggregation Problems

Electricity plays some role as an input in the production of almost every good. This role, however, is a double one. With size of industrial plant given, electricity input, like costs, has a fixed and a variable component. Electricity is used for lighting the plant, sometimes for heating, and for other minor uses the intensity of which does not vary with the size of the plant's output. Of course, this is only an approximation. Few costs and few inputs are truly constant. Overtime work, extra shifts, and the like may require more electricity for the above purposes when the plant's output becomes unusually large; furthermore, it is clear that at zero output the lights are turned off. Nevertheless, for normal operations the intensity of use of electricity for such purposes is relatively constant.

However, such uses are not the only ones which require electricity. Electric power is used to run various machines, and, in some industries, for various electro-chemical processes. These uses and the amount of electricity required for them do indeed vary with output. Indeed, in the absence of technological change one might very well argue that this part of the electricity input could be expected to be directly proportional to output, as substitutes for electricity in the production process are unlikely to be available without considerable outlay for a changeover in capital equipment.

It would thus seem that an analysis of the demand for electricity for industrial use could content itself with fitting functions of the form:

(4.1.1) $$D_{it} = A_i + B_i X_{it} + U_{it}$$

where D_{it} is total electricity used by the ith industrial establishment; X_{it} is the output of that plant; A_i and B_i are constant parameters;

and U_{it} is a random disturbance with the usual properties. Indeed, had we data on single establishments, and were firms typically single-product producers, (4.1.1) would be a good approximation. However, this is far from being the case. Moreover, even if it were, such an analysis would still be incomplete, for it would ignore the problem of the effect of electricity price on output size and on the composition of output among various products. It may be true that, given the output of each finely classified product in each establishment, the electricity used in its production is given by a relation such as (4.1.1), but to content ourselves with such an analysis would be to overlook the point that the cost of the electricity input may be one of the determinants of output size and composition.

We shall consider the problem of aggregation over establishments below, now we consider the problem of aggregation over *products*, of the consequences of the prevalence of multi-product firms.

The argument can be put best by considering the case of a multi-product firm whose total output is measured by an index with a fixed weight for each product. Let us further suppose that, to begin, the cost of the variable electricity input per unit of output is a different proportion of total variable costs per unit for each product. Now let the price of electricity per kilowatt hour rise by a given amount. Suppose that the corresponding rise in cost is completely and exactly compensated by being passed on to consumers as a rise in the price of the product. That rise will be highest for those products in which the proportion of variable electricity costs per unit to total variable unit costs is greatest. Unless there is a systematic tendency for these latter goods to be those for which demand is most inelastic (or unless the demand for all goods is perfectly inelastic), the quantity of those goods demanded will fall by a greater percentage than does the quantity demanded of less electricity-intensive items. The composition of output will thus tend to shift away from products with relatively large variable electricity inputs. Of course, the total output will also have fallen. Now, keeping the percentage composition of output the same, increase the output of all goods until the total output—as measured by the fixed weight index—is just equal to its initial value.

Now total output is the same as it was before the electricity price rise, but the shift in its composition means that total variable electricity input will be *less* than its initial value. There has been substitution in demand, rather than in production.

Furthermore, it is easy to see that the argument does not depend on the assumption that the increase in costs is passed along to the consumer. Suppose that no increase in product prices takes place. Then a shift in the composition of output will still take place, for the more electricity-intensive goods will have fallen in relative profitability and it will pay to produce relatively less of them than before. The argument now proceeds as before. There has been substitution among products even though not directly among inputs. The argument is similar regarding a fall in electricity price. It is of course conceivable that in some reasonably defined group of products the relative demand elasticities are systematically such as to negate or reverse the above tendency. It is thus possible that over-all price elasticity is zero or even positive for some groups; however, this will not be the general case. Note that long- and short-term adjustments must be distinguished.

It is thus inevitable (and indeed desirable) to look at fairly broadly defined commodity groups. In general, the greater the degree of aggregation over commodities, the greater the effect just noted. On the other hand, as usual, the greater the degree of aggregation, the less precision in the measurement of this or any other effect. Perhaps the most desirable grouping would be the three-digit industry of the Standard Industrial Classification; however, this sort of decision is taken out of our hands by the paucity of data available.

There is another problem of theory which must be considered. Many firms in heavy or even in light industry own electricity-generating equipment and do not take their full requirement or even an appreciable portion thereof from the public supply. Aside from the data problems created by this, a problem of valuation arises. The above argument spoke of the results of a rise in the price of electricity. In practice, however, it would appear that such price must be the price of electricity sold to, and not of electricity generated by the industry. Why then should the firm that purchases none of its electric power be affected by such price changes? The answer is that the rational accounting procedure for such a firm is to value its electricity input at the going price for purchased electricity and to make the same cost calculations as do other firms. It is true that when electricity demand falls purchased electricity goes first, as the self-generating firm makes virtual profits on its electricity-generating activities, but, in the period with which we shall be concerned, no collection of firms in our data operated solely on self-generated electricity, and some even occasionally sold electricity to the public supply. It follows that such self-generated electricity must be included in our aggregative variable at least so long as we are unable to separate the output of our industrial units into the output of firms purchasing electricity and the output of those generating it themselves. Even if the output of the latter is not affected in the same way as is that of the former by changes in the price of purchased electricity, the *total* output of the unit of observation will be affected thereby, and this is what will concern us.

Accordingly, the model we shall use for the single establishment is:

$$(4.1.2) \qquad\qquad D_{it} = A_i + B_i X_{it} P_{it}^{\pi_i} + U_{it}$$

where D_{it} is understood to mean *all* electricity used by the ith establishment; P_{it} is the real price of electricity to the establishment; X_{it} is an output index; and π_i is a parameter.

We turn now to aggregation over establishments. Let us adopt a measurement convention. For all establishments producing the same goods with a given electricity-using technology, the B_i and π_i will be assumed the same; the A_i, however, may vary with the size of the plant, as larger plants require more lighting, and so forth (the A_i may also vary with the type of lighting arrangement or for other reasons; we assume this away). We select the plant in our data with the smallest A_i—the smallest plant—and measure the size of other plants by the ratio of their A_i to the smallest one. This may or may not be a good measure of plant capacity. Over large ranges of plant size it is

not a good measure if lighting and other requirements are not proportional to capacity as is certainly the case. However, the size of establishments does not vary greatly within an industry, so we shall
take the ratio of the A_i as a measure of relative plant size and of capacity.

Now consider a set of establishments, I. Consider the minimum
size of plant—minimum A_i—in all the data on plants with the same
technology and products. By the convention just established, we may
think of I as consisting of many (not necessarily an integral number
of) plants of this size. Let that number at time t be N_{It} and let that
minimum A_i be A. Summing (4.1.2) for all establishments in I, we
have:

$$(4.1.3) \qquad D_{It} = N_{It}A + BX_{It}P_{It}^{\pi} + U_{It}$$

where (all summations being over all i in I):

$$(4.1.4) \qquad D_{It} = \Sigma\, D_{it}\,; \qquad X_{It} = \Sigma\, X_{it}\,; \qquad U_{It} = \Sigma\, U_{it}\,;$$

$$B = B_i, \quad \pi = \pi_i, \quad \text{and} \quad P_{It} = P_{it} \text{ for all } i \text{ in } I\,.$$

The last set of equalities is an additional assumption. It will suffice
that it hold approximately.

Finally, let the capacity output of the minimum-size plant be
$\bar{x}$ and let the capacity output of I at time t be $\bar{X}_{It}$. Then, approximately,

$$(4.1.5) \qquad N_{It} = \bar{X}_{It}/\bar{x}\,.$$

It follows that with fixed technology (*i.e.*, fixed B and π and fixed
A_i for given plant size), the long-run demand function for electricity
from I will be:

$$(4.1.6) \qquad D_{It} = (A/\bar{x} + BP_{It}^{\pi})X_{It} + U_{It}$$

as capacity is adjusted to output in the long run (so that $X_{It} = \bar{X}_{It}$).
Of course, changes in technology are far more important in determin-

ing long-run electricity input requirements, and we shall return to this below.

2. Estimating Procedures and Data

Now there are three types of possible observations on our variables. First, I in the above equations might be constant, but t might vary—a time series on some defined (but possibly growing) group of establishments. Second, the reverse might be the case—a cross-section of sets of establishments at the same time. Finally, both I and t might vary, giving us a moving cross-section, a rectangular block of data. Each of these cases raises special problems, and these we now consider.

The most straightforward estimating procedure arises when the observations are time series. First, suppose that the time series includes only years in which output was at capacity. Then (4.1.6) is the proper equation. However, unfortunately, (4.1.6) is not linear, nor will any transformation of the variables (that does not depend on knowing the parameters of (4.1.6)) make it so. Hence, β, π, and $A/\bar{x}$ must be estimated by some appropriate iterative and approximative technique. While these are available, they are computationally cumbersome. Furthermore, they are unsuited for application to short time series, for it is impossible to obtain any estimates of standard errors save asymptotic ones on the assumption that least-squares estimates are really maximum likelihood estimates. While this last assumption is generally present in any case, and while the probabilistic interpretation of standard errors is open to serious question in all econometric work, the fact that the estimates of standard errors under discussion are only asymptotic as the sample size grows means that no good estimate of the reliability of the obtained parameters can be obtained in a small sample.

Next, suppose that the time series contains some years in which output was below capacity; then there are two possibilities. Either capacity can be independently estimated, in which case (4.1.3) can be estimated by iterative techniques, or else no such estimates are available. In the latter case, either such years can be discarded or the assumption can be made that the growth in capacity over time is linear so that differencing (4.1.3) and estimating the resulting expression by iterative techniques eliminates the effect of the first term of (4.1.3) by placing it in the estimated constant term. However, if output is seriously below capacity, it is unreasonable to assume that capacity is growing steadily.

Now, all the above procedures lead to the use of iterative estimation techniques; hence, they require fairly large samples for their use. However, not only are such long time series not available (see below), but even if they were, they would be useless. It is of no avail to have many observations if they are not all generated by the mechanism being investigated,[1] and changes in technology will generally intervene in any time series of some length. Hence, estimation of our model from time-series data alone is not generally feasible.

Now consider the second type of data—cross-sections. Here the problem of small samples need not necessarily bother us, although iterative techniques will again be required. However, there are other problems. Our data, to be described below, are not for individual establishments but for all establishments in a given industry in selected states. Now, variations in capacity output (and hence in the first term of (4.1.3)) over *states* are the result of locational decisions made in the past. This has certain consequences. First, especially for industries with high electric power requirements—and these are the industries of greatest interest from our point of view—one important factor in such locational decisions is the availability of cheap power—the cost of electricity. Since geographical patterns in electricity price tend to be fairly constant over time, current electricity price is likely to be highly correlated over states with the electricity price that determined such decisions and hence with capacity output. It follows that one of the advantages usually possessed by cross-sections over time series, the reduction of multicollinearity, will be diminished here.

However, the location argument has more serious consequences than this. Just as the observations in a time series must all be gen-

---

[1] See FISHER, *A Priori Information and Time Series Analysis*, Amsterdam: North-Holland Publishing Co., 1962, Chapter 1, for a discussion of the implications of this.

erated by the same mechanism to be of any use, so must the observations in a cross-section. Had we observations on single product industries—or even on industries in which the same products were produced in each establishment—this would present no problem. However, this is not the case. In fact, we have observations only on industries producing at best related products. Here the assumptions of (4.1.4) only hold approximately and the individual plant parameters differ somewhat. What is important, however, is not that the aggregation of (4.1.3) is only approximate but that the macro-parameters, B and π, can be rather different for different states. Even this would create little problem were it likely to be the case that the distribution of these parameters over states is independent of the values of X_{It} and P_{It}. This, however, is most unlikely. The fact that technologically homogeneous sub-groups of firms in an industry tend to locate in a few states at most means that B is likely to be correlated with electricity price; the fact that location in industries with heavy power requirements is heavily influenced by the cost of power means that B will tend to be high in states where P_{It} is low. Further, given locations, the composition of outputs over states will still depend on P_{It}. This kind of dependence, however, means that estimates of all parameters over states will be rather uninterpretable, for this sort of variation will not be duplicated over time.[2]

---

[2] It is not true—as might seem tempting to suppose—that, if all other effects on location are distributed over states independently of the price of electricity, the effect over states of the latter variable is precisely the long-run price effect (technology constant) in which we are interested. The long-run composition of output in a state with a given price of electricity is not the same, other things being equal, as would be the composition of output in the nation as a whole in the long run for the same electricity price. An example will make this clear.

Suppose that every state initially has the same electricity price. Further, suppose that all states are identical in every relevant respect. Now let the price of electricity rise in State A. The composition of output in State A will shift toward less electricity-intensive goods and processes. So far, the adjustment might well be the same as would take place in all states if all electricity prices had risen by the same amount. However, since there is no reason to suppose that the demand for the electricity-intensive goods has fallen in the market area previously served by State A, the contraction of electricity in-

It follows that the use of cross-section data for our purposes requires a high degree of homogeneity in the data. It is not possible to suppose that the effects of inhomogeneity over firms will be randomly distributed over states; rather, such effects will be correlated with the parameters of interest and will alter them and our estimates of them, making our results more or less uninterpretable for purposes of prediction or explanation over time.

However, some information may be gleaned from cross-section data even where homogeneous data are not available. It is pointed out in the preceding footnote that the effects of differentials in electricity price on the geographic distribution of output compositions are likely to be greater than the effects over time, as the opportunities for geographic adjustment are greater than those for adjustment to a universal change in the real price of electricity. It follows that estimation of (4.1.6) for a full-capacity year from state cross-section data will yield an upper bound (absolutely) for π provided that technology has been reasonably constant for some time. This may be worthwhile having, if precise estimation of π is impossible.

------

tensive outputs (or the passing along to consumers of the rise in electricity price) will raise the prices of such goods relative to others in that market area. States other than A (most likely its neighbors) will now possess a comparative advantage in the production of electricity intensive goods and the composition of their output will ultimately shift to reflect this. There has been no change in their price of electricity, however, and, since electricity is sold at fixed rates, there will not be any in the short run. Moreover, since it is very doubtful indeed whether electric power production involves a rising marginal cost curve, there is little reason to expect price ever to change due to the increase in demand. Even if it did change upward, however, as more costly power sites came into use, the fact would remain that the composition of output in the neighboring states had shifted toward more electricity-intensive goods at the initial price or at a slightly higher one. It is thus not correct to suppose that adjustments over states and adjustments over time are ultimately the same. When the average price of electricity rises in the country as a whole, the alternative courses of action involve only shifts between goods and processes; however, when the price of electricity differs over states, there is the alternative of relocation or of geographical shifts in output composition.

This sort of problem is a common one in the use of cross-section estimates for time series prediction or explanation. See E. Kuh, "The Validity of Cross-Sectionally Estimated Behavior Equations in Time Series Applications," *Econometrica*, 27 (April, 1959), No. 2, pp. 197–214.

Further, B may be estimated under some circumstances. Let B_I be the value of B in the Ith state. Let $\bar{P}_t$ be a weighted average over I of the P_{It}, the weights being the quantity of electricity consumed by the industry in each state. Assume that the effects of differential electricity prices on the B_I can be represented by:

$$(4.2.1) \qquad B_I = C\,(P_{It}/\bar{P}_t)^\mu$$

where C and μ are constant parameters. (The addition of an error term here would, under appropriate assumptions, only mean that later estimates are consistent but not unbiased. This is a detail of little later importance.) Substituting in (4.1.6):

$$(4.2.2) \qquad D_{It} = AX_{It}/\bar{x} + CP_{It}^{\mu+\pi} X_{It}/\bar{P}_t^\mu + U_{It}\,.$$

Thus, C and B would always coincide if P_{It} were always at its weighted average value. Further, this is B, nationally. However, the estimate of C that is obtained from fitting (4.2.2) to cross-section data will in fact be an estimate of this common value and hence of the over-all B for the industry.[3] Note that μ here represents the effects *additional* to π of electricity price on geographic adjustments in output composition.

Of course, in practice, the assumptions behind (4.2.1) will only hold very approximately. Other factors—principally locational—affecting the composition of output may not be distributed independently of electricity price. However, this is a little beside the point, since no interpretation of (4.2.1) other than that it represents the *gross* effect of electricity price differentials—*i.e.*, including the effects of all such other factors—is intended. It is true, however, that the *form* which such gross effects take is unlikely to be more than approximately that of (4.2.1). Therefore only very crude estimation of B is possible.

The final type of observation is that of moving cross-sections. As the problems involved here are generally the same as those just discussed, we need not consider them.

Now unfortunately, the available data are not such as to meet our

---

[3] Note the analogy with the model of Chapter 1.

stringent requirements. Data are available at best for the two-digit industries of the Standard Industrial Classification. In time series, data which include self-generated electricity are only available for 1950–56 with the exception of 1953 from the *Annual Survey of Manufactures*. Even were two-digit industries homogeneous, and even if no iterative techniques were used, this would not be a sufficient number of observations.[4]

As for cross-section data, sufficient observations are available from the *Annual Survey of Manufactures for 1956* on ten two-digit industries by selected states for 1955 and 1956 and self-generated data can be estimated by assuming that the ratio of generated to purchased electricity is the same in every state. However, the two-digit industry is far from being homogeneous enough for cross-section work.[5] Hence no sophisticated estimation is here possible, and the techniques described above must be used to interpret the results.

Since only an upper (absolute) bound can be obtained for π and only crude estimates for B, it is pointless to go through the computational difficulty of an iterative technique. Multiply the first term of (4.2.2) by P_{It}^0, that is, by unity; then, as in Chapter 1, least-squares regression of log D_{It} on log X_{It} and log P_{It} will give estimates of weighted averages of $\mu + \pi$ and zero, and of C and $A/\bar{x}$. Formally, using a logarithmic regression, we estimate:

$$(4.2.3) \qquad D_{It} = K X_{It}^{\beta} P_{It}^{\alpha} + V_{It}$$

as an approximation to (4.2.2).

In (4.2.3), β is allowed to differ from unity because we shall be us-

---

[4] One other set of time series data is available, the data for all industry taken together in the "Large Light and Power" classification of the Federal Power Commission and reported by states by the Edison Electric Institute. While high correlations can be obtained here, the parameter estimates are meaningless, since, unlike the case of households, there is no sense in which states are reasonable groupings here.

[5] Examples of such geographic inhomogeneity are easy to think of. Chemicals or especially Primary Metal Industries which includes the electrolytic aluminum industry as well as non-electrolytic industries will serve.

ing value added by manufacture as our output index. As neither this index nor any other existing one is properly weighted for our purposes—*i.e.*, weighted by electricity inputs—it is entirely possible for β to be less than unity in cross-section data. This will occur if locational factors, uncorrelated with the price of electricity, cause parts of the two-digit industry being studied, which parts weigh heavily in the value added index, to locate in a few states and if such parts are those with relatively low electricity input coefficients. In such a case, the states with high value added will be those with relatively low electricity inputs so that D_{It} will go up less than proportionately with value added over states, even though it would have unit elasticity over time, given balanced growth in the two-digit industry. The reverse case—β greater than unity—is also possible, but somewhat unlikely, since, if the more important components of the value added index are also the electricity intensive parts of the industry, their location is likely to be influenced by the price of electricity. The example of Industry 33, Primary Metal Industries, should make this clear. The biggest component of value added is here iron and steel; locational factors are obviously not directly related to electricity prices for this component; finally, iron and steel is not the largest electricity user relative to output in the industry. Accordingly, we find a β significantly less than one, below. Clearly, however, had the relative weights given to iron and steel and to aluminum in the value added index been reversed, we should find a β close to one, as the location of alumina reduction plants is very much influenced by power costs.

One more word on this subject is in order. If β does differ from unity, it is clear that the interpretation of α in (4.2.3) remains unchanged. It is the maximum, over-all price effect. However, it is not clear how to interpret estimates of K arrived at from cross-section data. It is unreasonable to suppose that an equation similar to (4.2.1) relates the true value of K over time and the K in (4.2.3), for it is clear that differences in X_{It} over states have no effect of themselves on output composition. Therefore, when β is very different from unity, estimates of K cannot be taken as estimates of the input-output coefficient for the entire two-digit industry (although we shall see below that something more than this can be said).

We now discuss the interpretation of the parameters of (4.2.3) in terms of those of (4.2.2) on the assumption that β is unity. Ignore error terms, and equate the right-hand sides of both expressions. Solve the resulting equation for P_{It}^{α}, obtaining:

$$(4.2.4) \qquad P_{It}^{\alpha} = \frac{P_{It}^{0}(AX_{It}/\bar{x}) + P_{It}^{\mu+\pi}(CX_{It}/\bar{P}_{t}^{\mu})}{KX_{It}}.$$

If we now adopted a measurement convention, similar to that of Chapter 1, of measuring P_{It} as a multiple of $\bar{P}_{t}$, and adjusted C anp K accordingly by multiplying them by $\bar{P}_{t}^{\pi}$ and $\bar{P}_{t}^{\alpha}$, respectively, only an apparent change, we should find that α must be such as to make P_{It}^{α} a weighted average of 0 and $\mu + \pi$, the weights being the quantities of electricity used for constant and for variable purposes, respectively, at the average price of electricity. Approximately, then, we can regard α as an average of 0 and $\mu + \pi$ with those same weights[6] and can tabulate $\mu + \pi$ for given α and relative importance of con-

---

[6] Thus, dropping subscripts, let r be any number $1 \geq r \geq 0$. Let

(A) $\qquad P^{\alpha} = rP^{0} + (1-r)P^{\mu+\pi}.$

Expand each term in (A) in MacLaurin series and ignore terms of higher than first degree. Thus:

(B) $\qquad P^{\alpha} = P^{0} + \alpha P^{0} \log P$

(C) $\qquad P^{0} = P^{0}$

(D) $\qquad P^{\mu+\pi} = P^{0} + (\mu + \pi)P^{0} \log P.$

Substituting into (A) and solving for α, we have;

(E) $\qquad \alpha = \dfrac{rP^{0} + (1-r)P^{0} - P^{0} + (1-r)(\mu+\pi)P^{0} \log P}{P^{0} \log P}$

$\qquad\qquad = r(0) + (1-r)(\mu + \pi)$

so that α is approximately the same weighted average of 0 and $\mu + \pi$ a P^{α} is of P^{0} and $P^{\mu+\pi}$, as claimed in the text.

stant and variable use. Since $\mu + \pi$ is only a rough limit, anyway, the approximations here involved are not too important.

Similarly, using the same technique, K can be seen to be the sum of $A/\bar{x}$ and C, and these can also be crudely tabulated.

However, as in Chapter 1, it is the parameters actually estimated which are of greatest interest. K is essentially an average long-run input-output coefficient and α indicates the way in which that coefficient is affected by electricity price. As technological change is likely to make any precise estimation of our model somewhat fatuous, it is desirable to have easily obtainable estimates of such over-all parameters so that we can see in what direction technological change proceeds. We shall return to this in the last section.

Finally, given an estimate of K (note that β must be unity here), another estimate of π (or its over-all approximation) is available in principle. We can take for each industry the national total of value added and multiply it by K. Dividing the product into total electricity consumption and finding the log of the resulting quotient to the base of the average price of electricity to the industry gives an estimate of over-all price elasticity. We thus use cross-section estimates as *a priori* information in dealing with the national total. However, the interpretation of such estimates is difficult. It is not clear whether they are short- or long-run, and they are subject to serious error as we shall be ignoring all error effects. They might be of interest, nonetheless, especially when compared with our cross-sectionally estimated values for α—theoretically their (absolute) upper bounds. When β is not unity so that our cross-sectionally estimated K is unreliable, we may still find K as a function of over-all π or the reverse by the same method. In this way, educated guesses as to one of the two parameters help to fix the value of the other. Unfortunately, application of this method to our data yields widely varying and unreliable results of little interest.

A few notes about the data are necessary before proceeding to the results. Price is taken as average cost per kilowatt hour of purchased electricity (the actual units for all variables are given in the next section). The analysis is performed for 1956 (1955 would differ only negligibly) for the two-digit industries and there is no correction by price index (as none is necessary). The independent variables are thus in 1956 prices.[7]

Aside from the manufacturing industries which are of most interest, similar cross-section data by states are available for some of the extractive industries for 1954 from the *1954 Census of Mineral Industries*. The quantity of electricity here consumed is far less than in manufacturing, but we include the results for the sake of completeness. As data are here available for three- or even four-digit industries, and as the peculiar characteristics of the extractive industries make locational responses to electricity price differentials somewhat difficult (although, given location, shifts in output composition are still possible), over-all π probably lies near its estimated upper bound here. However, 1954 was not a full capacity year, so that the constant part of (4.2.2) will receive too heavy a weight in the averages, pulling α too far towards zero.

3. The Results

Table 4.3.1 gives the results of estimation of the logarithmic form of (4.2.3) on the indicated data for the two-digit manufacturing industries (results for the extractive industries are given below). As stated, all values are in 1956 prices. Electricity consumption is in millions of kilowatt hours; output is measured by millions of dollars of value added; electricity price is in cents per kilowatt hour. The values of α and β given are independent of this choice of units—they are elasticities. The value of K given is not thus independent. For β approximately unity, it may be interpreted as the number of kilowatt hours consumed per dollar of value added when electricity price is one cent per kilowatt hour. As the actual electricity prices ob-

---

[7] To some extent, (4.2.1) would be more plausible if some long-term—*i.e.,* time average—measure of electricity price were used. We do not have the data for this, however. Geographical differentials in electricity price are reasonably constant.

TABLE 4.3.1 INDUSTRY REGRESSIONS: TWO-DIGIT INDUSTRIES, 1956

Industry	α	β	K	R^2	Degrees of Freedom	β Significantly Different from Unity
20 Food and Kindred Products	—0.7841 (0.4065)	+ 0.6591[aaa] (0.1324)	12.88	.8323[aaa]	11	YES
22 Textile Mill Products	—1.6167[aaa] (0.1117)	+ 1.0071[aaa] (0.0877)	2.84	.9880[aaa]	6	NO
26 Pulp, Paper, and Products	—0.9747[a] (0.2077)	+ 0.7203 (0.4205)	26.43	.8822[a]	3	NO
28 Chemicals and Products	—2.5976[aaa] (0.5234)	+ 0.6150[a] (0.2167)	22.55	.6387[aaa]	14	NO
32 Stone, Clay, and Glass Products	—1.7386 (1.2231)	+ 1.0273[a] (0.3074)	2.44	.8429	3	NO
33 Primary Metal Industries	—1.2829[aaa] (0.2117)	+ 0.4937[aaa] (0.1188)	9.17	.7428[aaa]	16	YES
34 Fabricated Metal Products	+ 0.5533 (0.4832)	+ 1.1094[aaa] (0.1143)	0.29	.9593[aaa]	4	NO
	—	+ 1.1009[aaa] (0.1175)	0.39	.9460[aaa]	5	NO
35 Machinery, Except Electrical	—1.3349[a] (0.4286)	+ 0.9043[aaa] (0.0870)	1.30	.9742[aaa]	7	NO
36 Electrical Machinery	—1.8209[a] (0.4489)	+ 0.3797 (0.2191)	76.50	.8985[a]	4	YES
37 Transportation Equipment	+ 0.6877 (0.6445)	+ 1.0526[aaa] (0.1174)	0.61	.9521[aaa]	5	NO
	—	+ 0.9859[aaa] (0.1005)	1.04	.9412[aaa]	6	NO

[a] Significant at five per cent level.
[aa] Significant at one per cent level.
[aaa] Significant at one-tenth of one per cent level.

served are in this neighborhood, this is a sensible choice of units.[8]
Note that this interpretation is *not* possible where β is considerably
under unity. Where the sign of α is positive, we give the regression
with log X_{It} as the only independent variable as well as the full
results.

We observe several items. First, there is a significantly negative
price effect in six of our ten industries and a non-significantly negative effect observed in two more. Values of β are all positive and are
significant in all but two industries. Further, β is non-significantly
different from unity in seven industries and significantly different in
the remaining three. Of the former seven, β is within about ten per
cent of unity in five. There does not seem to be any particular relation between high or low α and β far from unity. However, as expected, the only values of β which are far from unity are less than
that figure, not greater.

Moreover, we observe an elastic price effect in six industries. It is
difficult to know how to interpret this result. On the one hand, our
estimates must err on the side of too great elasticity, since, as remarked in the last section, they include the effects of geographic adjustment. Perhaps it is thus indicative that we did not obtain more
elastic results. On the other hand, observed elasticity is sometimes
quite high. Furthermore, while our estimates overestimate the over-
all elasticity of demand, they underestimate the upper (absolute)
limit on π—the elasticity of the demand for electricity for variable
uses. Rough estimates of that limit may be obtained from Table
4.3.1 by multiplying each α by the reciprocal of the percentage of
electricity used for variable purposes. It seems unlikely that such
percentage is ever above ninety-five or below fifty per cent. Hence,
our numbers underestimate $\mu + \pi$ in absolute value by about five

---

[8] To convert to other units is fairly simple. If electricity consumption is
to be multiplied by some constant, the given value of K must also be multiplied by that constant. If output is multiplied by a constant, Z, K must be
divided by Z^β and similarly for price. Thus, for example, if P_{It} is to be expressed in multiples of $\bar{P}_t$ as suggested in the last section, K must be multiplied by $\bar{P}_t{}^\alpha$. As indicated in the text, the present system of units seems as
convenient for interpretation of K as any other.

and one-third to one hundred per cent (where meaningful, the same remarks apply to our estimates of K). Probably the degree of under-estimation is least where our estimates show greatest elasticity as these are perhaps the industries with greatest relative variable use of electricity, but it is difficult to be sure on this point. The most that can be said is that there is probably a fairly high price elasticity of demand—given 1956 technology—for electricity in the long run in several industries. However, it is also the case that the ten observed industries are probably those with the greatest price elasticity of electricity demand.

It is difficult to say whether the observed pattern of elasticities over industries is a plausible one. We believe that it is. On the one hand, a two-digit industry with uniformly low electricity input coefficients should show low price elasticity of electricity demand; on the other hand, the same should be true of any two-digit industry with uniformly high or uniformly medium electricity input coefficients, as, with value added held constant, output composition—and hence electricity requirements—will be uninfluenced by electricity price in such cases. The greatest price elasticity should thus occur in the industry with the greatest differentials in electricity input coefficients, provided that such differentials occur between two or more goods that are fairly close substitutes either in production or in consumption. To some extent, the chemical industry seems to have these characteristics more than any other in our data and it is this industry which shows by far the greatest price elasticity of electricity demand.

This brings us to the last point which requires discussion before leaving the constant technology model. We said in the first section that aggregate industries—such as the two-digit industries—are desirable units of observation, not because they are homogeneous, but because the price effects we desire to observe are the consequence of adjustments in the composition of output among different processes and goods. While the use of broad aggregates is undesirable for other reasons, it is desirable for this one. The question now remains: are the observed effects of electricity price (however imperfectly estimated) the principal or only effects, or are there other effects as across the board changes in power costs affect the composition of national output among rather than within the two-digit industries? Fortunately, the answer seems reasonably clear and has been indicated in the last paragraph. Electricity-cost-induced changes in output composition can come about in two ways or in a combination of them. First, cost increases can be passed along to the consumer and substitution can occur in the consumption of final output. Second, some processes or the production of some goods can become more costly relative to others and there can thus be substitution in production. In the long run, either possibility will result in shifts of capital from the production of some goods to the production of others.

Now there are two points to be made. First, suppose that, with all other prices remaining constant, the price of electricity used in the manufacture of two goods rises by the same percentage and that such cost increase is wholly passed along to the consumer. Further, suppose that the input and cost structure of the two goods are not the same so that the price of good A, the electricity intensive good, rises by a greater percentage than does the price of good B. Since all goods are in the budget of the consumer, there will be some effect on relative demand for the two goods, whatever they are, through income effects. However, if the two goods are entirely unrelated, it seems unlikely that such effects will be large. Of course, if each has other substitutes, there will be shifts in relative demand elsewhere. However, there will be no particularly large direct effect on the relative demand for goods A and B themselves. This situation is quite different, however, when A and B are close substitutes for each other. Then not only will demand for them fall relative to other goods, there will be a reaction in the relative demands for the two goods themselves. On our assumptions, good B will be substituted for good A and for the same value added output, demand for electricity will be less. This sort of price-of-electricity effect seems likely to be considerably more important than that in the previous case.

Now let the price of electricity rise by the same percentage amount in all industries. Let such price rises be passed on (through differing cost structures) to the consumer. Ignoring any effect on the total size of output—which we wish to hold constant—we consider only effects on its composition. In view of the foregoing, it seems clear that the important effects here will be direct substitution ones. Less electricity-intensive goods will be substituted for more electricity-intensive goods serving the same or similar ends. However—rather crudely it is true—the boundaries of a two-digit industry represent a large break in the chain of substitution; two goods in the same two-digit industry are likely to be much better substitutes for each other than are two goods in different two-digit industries, at least as a general approximation. Therefore, the electricity price effects which we have investigated are likely to be the principal ones so far as effects on demand are concerned.

Second, we consider the changes in output composition that can stem from a differential cost increase due to a rise in electricity price. Here the analysis is a little different, although there are points of similarity to the demand case. Let us return to the case where electricity price changes affect only two goods. If capital flowed freely from one industry to another—if there were perfect and quick entry into, and exit out of all lines of production—then it would obviously be the case that the effect of an electricity price rise on the relative output of two goods would depend only on the change in their relative profitability. Investment would flow, as it were, from the more electricity-intensive to the less electricity-intensive good. In the very long run, this would probably still be the case in fact with fixed technology. In the meantime, however, the relative adjustment will be made very slowly if the two goods are not related in some way (substitutes in production). Production of good A—the electricity-intensive good—will be cut back and production of other goods by the same firms increased; however, the same will be true of good B. It is far from obvious that any moderately long (or even any finite) period will see such effects result in the adjustment in relative output of the two goods that would take place in a perfect capital market with free entry and exit everywhere. On the other hand, if A and B are substitutes in production, the situation will be different. If they can be produced with the same equipment with little changeover cost, there will be an immediate effect on their relative output in favor of B. If they are produced by the same firm but in different plants, such an effect will also occur, but it will be less immediate; it will take time for the firm to spin off capacity (more of the A plant than of the B plant will ultimately be sold or scrapped). Finally, if they are produced by different firms but with related technology, there will still be a direct effect in a moderate time as experienced firms shift from A to B (remember that the total output of the two goods, as measured by some index of production such as value added, is fixed).

Now let there be a universal electricity price rise of some given per cent. Let this not be passed on to consumers and consider the results when aggregate output is at its former value (as measured by some index). The adjustments which would take place immediately in the relative outputs of various goods in a world of free exit and entry will take place fastest in the real world where firms exiting from, or cutting back on production and capacity of more electricity-intensive goods find it easiest to enter the production of less electricity-intensive goods. Indeed, the availability of profitable alternatives in a closely related line will make it easier to exit from a less profitable (more electricity-intensive) one. However, as before, it is roughly correct to say that it is easier to move from one part of a given two-digit industry to another than to cross the boundaries of the two-digit industries. The two-digit industries are composed of firms producing the same or similar goods with the same or similar technology, and, while the similarities are not always very great, they are generally greater than the similarities between goods and technologies in different two-digit industries. Therefore, at least in the only moderately long run, electricity-price-induced adjustments in the composition of output within two-digit industries are likely to be more important than similar inter-industry adjustments. The effects which we have investigated again turn out to be the important ones.

Finally, the analysis just given is not a substitute for the discussion of demand effects, it is a complement. Differential effects on demand result in differential changes in profitability and our analysis of the case of response to these goes along with our discussion of where large relative demand effects are likely to occur. It follows that our conclusion that the intra-two-digit industry effects of a given electricity price change are likely to be a great deal more important than the inter-industry effects is strengthened.[9]

This completes our discussion of the constant technology case save for the results for the extractive industries. These latter results are

TABLE 4.3.2 INDUSTRY REGRESSION: EXTRACTIVE INDUSTRIES, 1954

Industry	α	β	K	R^2	Degrees of Freedom	β Significantly Different from Unity
1011 Iron Ores	—0.5004 (0.9488)	+0.8503[aa] (0.1791)	7.67	.8620[a]	4	NO
1032 – 1034 Lead and Zinc Ores	—0.8849[aa] (0.2544)	+0.7493[aaa] (0.0954)	11.43	.8926[aaa]	9	YES
1211 – 1213 Bituminous Coal	—0.3462 (0.3579)	+0.9695[aaa] (0.0552)	3.24	.9599[aaa]	13	NO
1312 – 1313 Crude Petroleum and Natural Gas	—1.8567 (1.0718)	+0.6524[aaa] (0.1286)	6.20	.7890[aaa]	12	YES
1441 Sand and Gravel	—0.9096[aaa] (0.1933)	+0.8010[aaa] (0.0993)	5.33	.7927[aaa]	18	NO
1420 Crushed and Broken Stone	—1.0710[a] (0.4876)	+0.9620[aaa] (0.1697)	4.82	.7280[aaa]	12	NO

[a] Significant at five per cent level.
[aa] Significant at one per cent level.
[aaa] Significant at one-tenth of one per cent level.

[9] This discussion has ignored the possibility that electricity demand in one industry—e.g., fabricated metal products—can fall because of a rise in electricity price in an input producing industry—e.g., primary metals—which raises costs. Such effects seem likely to be very small, however.

presented in Table 4.3.2. All values here are in 1954 prices, otherwise the remarks preceding Table 4.3.1 apply to them with the addition of the observations made at the end of the last section. All observations with less than ten million kilowatt hours of purchased electricity have been deleted to avoid large errors in the computation of electricity price due to rounding.

By and large, the results here are as expected. Price elasticities are closer to zero and less significant than for manufacturing. As argued in the last section, this is due both to the greater geographic homogeneity of the extractive industries, and to the fact that 1954 was not a full-capacity year. Since these facts together mean that α is quite possibly biased downward, these results may be taken as further indication that long-run electricity demand from industry is somewhat price sensitive, given constant technology.[10]

4. Technological Change

So far, our discussion has proceeded entirely in terms of a constant technological structure, and our results have been interpreted on that basis. In fact, of course, the assumption of unchanging technology is not justified as a basis for an analysis of the demand for electricity. Our previous analysis must therefore be taken as showing *tendencies*: as giving some indications of what would happen in the long run if technology did remain unchanged. We must now directly concern ourselves with technological change. Even in the preceding sections the data were such as to severely limit the results; the data on technological change are even more limited (to some extent it is even difficult to recognize such data). Perhaps worse than this, there is simply no adequate analysis of the mechanism of technological change. We know very little in this area and the ensuing discussion of historical change in the postwar period will hardly scratch the surface.

---

[10] As electricity prices are greater than one cent per kilowatt hour here in general, our estimates of K are somewhat larger than the corresponding directly observed input coefficients.

Probably the best over-all measure of technological change for our purposes is the comparison of two over-all electricity input coefficients (K) for the same industry at different points in time under the same price conditions. This is not an easy thing to observe, but we can attempt it. Data are available on total electricity inputs for two-digit industries from the *Census of Manufactures* for 1939, 1947, and 1954; and from the *Survey of Manufactures* for various other years. Data on electricity generated by private industry were not collected before 1939.[11] We choose to look at 1947 and 1956, as these are the two farthest spaced full capacity years for which data are available. Moreover, 1956 is the year covered in the results of the last section and this will be convenient later.

We wish to investigate the question of the relation, if any, between the importance of power costs in total costs and the direction and magnitude of change in the electricity input coefficient. We ask whether those two-digit industries in which electricity costs are relatively important tend to experience technological change—or to work to induce such change—reducing that importance to a greater extent than those industries where electricity costs are relatively less important. This is not the only question that we might ask—nor is it necessarily the one of most interest; however, it is one on which we may be able to say something. Thus, for example, it would be very interesting and valuable to be able to say whether technological change which reduces the importance of electricity proceeds faster in the same industry—other things being equal—when electricity price is high or low, rising or falling, rising faster or rising slower, and so forth. Unfortunately, not only is it unclear how to keep "other things equal"—although we might be willing to attempt this—but also we do not have data covering an adequate period before 1947 with which to compare changes in the postwar period (as already observed, 1939 was not a full capacity year and data on self-generated electricity

---

[11] Indeed, data on three-digit industries are available for the census years; however, we cannot use those years except for 1947, since they were not full capacity years. Furthermore, we have no information on fixed-technology electricity price effects save for two-digit industries.

were not collected before this; further, technological change during the war years is obviously likely to be rather special). At most, in addition to our original question, we shall be able to give some indication of the general direction which technological change has taken since the war.

We thus examine the percentage changes in national over-all electricity input coefficients from 1947 to 1956 for the two-digit industries. This examination raises two preliminary questions. First, we shall try to take account of electricity price effects not affecting technological change, using the results of the last section; the question remains, however, of the extent to which we are justified in attributing any remaining changes in the input coefficient to technological change. Clearly, such changes can come about through changes in the composition of industry output not induced by electricity price. It would seem that what we are calling technological change is really a *mélange* which includes exogenous changes in taste. To a large extent this is true, but the objection is not justified in the form in which we have just stated it. If we think about large changes in the relative demand for the products making up a two-digit industry's output, it is clear that major shifts are themselves the results of technological change—of the discovery of new goods or of improvement in the quality of old ones; of new and cheaper processes leading to changes in relative prices, and so forth. Of course, exogenous (*i.e.*, independent of technological change) shifts in demand certainly took place, but it seems clear that the major shifts have been due to technological factors. Besides, exogenous demand shifts may be randomly distributed over all industries.

On the other hand, there is a sense in which we are not interested in the effects of all technological change. We should like to be able to say whether high relative electricity costs tend to lead to technological change reducing the importance of electricity. When we look at historical coefficients, however, we are looking at the gross effects of all change. To the extent that electricity-intensive goods tend to be relatively new goods and thus relatively fast growing goods, the gross effect of technological change may be in the direction of greater electricity intensity, even if the effect just mentioned is in the opposite direction. It is thus difficult to observe the latter effect. It follows that if we do observe it at all, even non-significantly, it is likely to be present, but it is hard to be sure about this.

The second question points to a second source of error which, if it exists, tends to bias our results in the opposite direction. We are looking at percentage changes in input coefficients. There may be some sense, however, in which this is incorrect. Technological change may take the form rather of given absolute increases in the electricity coefficient per unit time. If this is true, then we shall be making a comparison which understates the relative change in those industries where electricity was already an important input in 1947. Further, there may be some sense in which those industries were near the (perhaps slowly moving) upper limit of their electricity input coefficients as a result of past technological change. In some sense industries that were highly electrified in 1947 may not have had the same opportunity for electricity-intensive technological change as did other industries. If this is the case, it means that our results in some sense overemphasize the effect for which we seek.

However, we do not believe that this is an important argument, although it is difficult to be certain. If only through the growth of already known goods, all industries had ample opportunity to experience changes in their electricity input coefficients in an upward direction. Further, the argument, even if true, does not mean that our results are not of interest; it means rather that the interpretation thereof is a little uncertain. Again, we are observing a gross rather than a net effect and it is best to be cautious about predicting therefrom. Indeed, it is far from certain that technological change is a subject about which any prediction is possible in our present state of knowledge.

With all these limitations in mind, we proceed to the results. The electricity input coefficients used are the total electricity inputs divided by the Federal Reserve Index of manufacturing production for the various industries. As we are interested in percentage changes over time, there is no difficulty in the fact that while these are essentially indices of value added, they are expressed in base year, price-corrected units. Our cost coefficients are the ratio of total electricity cost (imputing the cost of self-generated electricity) to value of shipments in 1947.[12]

TABLE 4.4.1 UNADJUSTED CHANGES IN ELECTRICITY INPUT COEFFICIENTS AND IMPORTANCE OF ELECTRIC POWER COSTS: TWO-DIGIT INDUSTRIES, 1947–56

Industry	$\dfrac{\text{EIC}^a-1956}{\text{EIC}^a-1947}$	1947 Cost Ratio	Rank- Col. (2)	Rank- Col. (3)
(1)	(2)	(3)	(4)	(5)
28 Chemicals and Products	2.8959	.00989	1	5
39 Miscellaneous Manufactures	2.1912	.00471	2	13
24 Lumber and Wood Products	1.7160	.00635	3	7
21 Tobacco Manufactures	1.6308	.00119	4	20
33 Primary Metal Industries	1.4452	.01318	5	3
25 Furniture and Fixtures	1.4369	.00456	6	14
20 Food and Kindred Products	1.4150	.00360	7	17
31 Leather and Leather Goods	1.3928	.00287	8	18
23 Apparel and Related Products	1.3602	.00184	9	19
34 Fabricated Metal Products	1.3460	.00515	10	9
38 Instruments and Related Products	1.3275	.00404	11	16
22 Textile Mill Products	1.3215	.00824	12	6
29 Petroleum and Coal Products	1.2460	.00492	13	10
35 Machinery, Except Electrical	1.1905	.00486	14	11
37 Transportation Equipment	1.1567	.00602	15	8
26 Pulp, Paper, and Products	1.1163	.01767	16	2
32 Stone, Clay, and Glass Products	1.0944	.01883	17	1
30 Rubber Products	0.9656	.01070	18	4
36 Electrical Machinery	0.9292	.00474	19	12
27 Printing and Publishing	0.8893	.00421	20	15

ᵃ Electricity Input Coefficient.

---

[12] Value of shipments for a two-digit industry includes considerable double counting as intra-industry shipments are counted. The coefficients given are therefore not a good measure of the importance of the price of electricity in the value of final products. (Such a measure would require knowledge of the internal input-output structure of the industry.) They do roughly measure the importance of power costs relative to all other gross costs for the average firm, and this is what is wanted here.

Table 4.4.1 presents these two sets of numbers for all two-digit industries and ranks the industries by each. So far, no attempt has been made to take account of the possible constant-technology effects of falling real electricity price.

We observe the following. First, three out of the twenty two-digit industries experienced a downward shift in electricity input coefficient between 1947 and 1956. Since no attempt has yet been made to eliminate the effects (with constant technology) of the falling real price of electricity, and since such effects would tend to raise the input coefficient, this must be considered the minimum number of two-digit industries experiencing technological change reducing the absolute importance of electricity.

Second, the Kendall τ coefficient of rank correlation between the last two columns is $- .1421$ which is not significant.[13] There is thus a tendency, although an insignificant one, for industries with highest relative electricity costs to experience least upward percentage shifts in their electricity input coefficient, if no account is taken of the constant-technology effects of electricity price changes.

We must now attempt to take account of such effects. In the last section we estimated the maximum electricity price effect for the technology (and the history) of 1956 for ten two-digit industries. We use those results by computing the percentage change for each industry in electricity price (in 1956 prices)[14] from 1947 to 1956 and multiplying the result by our estimate of α (where α was positive, we assume it zero). This gives the maximum percentage change in the electricity input coefficient which can be attributed to the change in electricity price to the industry on the assumption of no technological change. We accordingly adjust our observed 1947 coefficients by this percen-

---

[13] We use this instead of the Spearman coefficient previously employed because the sampling distribution of the latter is not known for number of ranks between 9 and 25.

[14] For industry 20, we used the wholesale price index of all commodities as a deflator; for all other industries, we used the index of all non-agricultural commodities.

tage and compute the effect of technological change from this new base. The results are presented in Table 4.4.2.

We observe the following. First, Kendall's τ for the last two columns is $-.1333$, which is not significant. The results in this respect are essentially unchanged from the previous case.[15] However, whereas

TABLE 4.4.2 ADJUSTED CHANGES IN ELECTRICITY INPUT COEFFICIENTS AND IMPORTANCE OF ELECTRIC POWER COSTS: TWO-DIGIT INDUSTRIES, 1947–56

Industry (1)	Adjusted Input Coef.- 1947 / Actual Input Coef.- 1947 (2)	Input Coef.- 1956 / Adjusted Input Coef.- 1947 (3)	Rank- Col. (3) (4)	1947 Cost- Ratio Rank (5)
28 Chemicals and Products	2.1467	1.3490	1	4
34 Fabricated Metal Products	1.0000	1.3460	2	7
20 Food and Kindred Products	1.0589	1.3363	3	10
33 Primary Metal Industries	1.2178	1.1867	4	3
37 Transportation Equipment	1.0000	1.1567	5	6
22 Textile Mill Products	1.3429	0.9841	6	5
35 Machinery, Except Electrical	1.2363	0.9648	7	8
26 Pulp, Paper, and Products	1.1693	0.9547	8	2
32 Stone, Clay, and Glass Products	1.2460	0.8784	9	1
36 Electrical Machinery	1.2363	0.7516	10	9

Table 4.4.1 showed only one of these ten industries and three out of the full set of twenty experiencing a decline in the electricity input coefficient, Table 4.4.2 shows fully half of the ten industries experiencing such a decline. Since the electricity price effects accounted for in deriving the latter results were maximum effects, the truth probably lies somewhere between the two. Between one and five

---

[15] Tests of cruder hypotheses than that of related ranks give about the same result (*e.g.*, tests that the probability of an item in the bottom half of the cost-ratio rank being in the top half of the technological-change rank is different from the same probability for items in the top half of the cost-ratio rank).

of these ten industries and between three and ten of the full twenty[16] experienced technological changes in this period tending to reduce the importance of electricity. On balance, technological change was either neutral or acted to increase the importance of electricity for industry as a whole.

---

[16] The number here is probably less than ten, since, to the extent that our results show a tendency to smaller increases (greater declines) in the electricity input coefficient in those industries where electricity is an important input, the ten industries of Table 4.4.1 are probably weighted toward declines.

APPENDICES

APPENDIX A

AGGREGATION OF INDIVIDUAL DEMAND FUNCTIONS

Let j indicate the individual household and let there be J households. We suppose that functions similar to the demand functions (1.1.11) and (1.1.12) hold for each household, *i.e.*:

(A.1)
$$D_{ijt} = C_{ij}(P_{jt}/\bar{P}_j)^{\alpha_{ij}}(Y_{jt}/\bar{Y}_j)^{\beta_{ij}}W_{ijt}$$

(A.2)
$$D_{jt} = \sum_{i=1}^{n}D_{ijt}.$$

We desire to consider certain aspects of aggregation over households.

It will simplify matters to assume P_{jt} the same for all j and t, but this is not a necessary restriction. Consider the aggregate equation obtained from (A.1) by dropping the j subscripts (this is essentially (1.1.11)). For this to hold together with (A.1), we must have:

(A.3)
$$C_i(P_t/\bar{P})^{\alpha_i}(Y_t/\bar{Y})^{\beta_i}W_{it} = \sum_{j=1}^{J}C_{ij}(P_{jt}/\bar{P}_j)^{\alpha_{ij}}(Y_{jt}/\bar{Y}_j)^{\beta_{ij}}W_{ijt}.$$

Now, let P_{jt}, P_t, Y_{jt}, and Y_t equal their respective averages. Then C_i is seen to be a weighted average of the C_{ij}, with the weights being the individual white good holdings. Further, similar to the discussion of (1.1.13) as an approximation to (1.1.12), it can be seen that β_i must move so as to make the term in Y_t a weighted average of the corresponding terms in Y_{jt}, the weights being the electricity consumption of the individual households' white good holdings. Similar remarks apply to α_i.

It is thus easy to see (by considering the case where all the β_{it} are equal) that if Y_t is to be a linear function of the Y_{jt}, the best function to use is not the sum, but a weighted average. Indeed, if all the β_{ij} were near unity, it would be clear that the proper weights were the same as those just mentioned. Even if this is not the case, some such average must be called for, probably one very close to this one.

Now, we may aggregate over white goods after aggregation over individuals (essentially as in Chapter 1) or before the latter aggregation. Aggregation over white goods in the latter case involves approximating (A.1) by the individual analogue of (1.1.13). Aggregation over individuals is then the same as before, save that a composite white good is used.

It is thus clear that some average income must be used in estimating (1.1.13). An average which weighted individual incomes by individual composite white good stocks would undoubtedly be a good one to use. Unfortunately, such an average is far from being available. Hence we use per capita income instead.

153

APPENDIX B

CONSUMERS' STOCKS BY STATES OF SELECTED MAJOR APPLIANCES, 1944–57*

TABLE B.1 CONSUMERS' STOCKS BY STATES: ELECTRIC DRYERS, 1946–57

Year	Maine	New Hamphire	Vermont	Massa-chusetts	Rhode Island	Con-necticut
1946	110	68	59	904	141	607
1947	339	209	181	2,789	436	1,873
1948	724	415	342	4,400	704	2,983
1949	976	516	409	4,976	1,086	3,627
1950	2,092	1,185	624	9,846	2,416	6,253
1951	3,210	2,017	841	17,700	4,650	11,098
1952	4,091	2,884	1,187	27,055	6,714	18,307
1953	5,454	4,012	1,688	40,415	8,560	25,897
1954	7,870	5,603	2,401	57,133	11,912	36,011
1955	12,856	8,594	4,216	82,352	15,263	50,192
1956	18,682	11,724	6,327	109,699	18,638	66,462
1957	23,398	13,832	8,225	130,172	20,691	77,143

Year	New York	New Jersey	Pennsyl-vania	Ohio	Indiana	Illinois
1946	2,450	978	2,166	1,756	923	2,267
1947	7,559	3,018	6,682	5,417	2,848	6,994
1948	14,818	4,190	14,451	11,628	6,795	12,400
1949	17,940	5,641	21,300	21,030	10,964	18,043
1950	35,538	12,158	47,085	52,054	23,085	40,763
1951	66,966	22,904	90,449	112,123	42,700	78,473
1952	102,132	35,514	139,172	189,258	70,753	122,559
1953	148,985	49,282	194,802	268,548	106,374	176,974
1954	201,956	65,871	258,976	360,509	152,426	239,415
1955	279,853	100,839	364,485	494,465	219,800	331,298
1956	370,526	136,813	500,784	629,874	287,554	428,130
1957	437,067	162,893	579,417	706,024	332,992	499,510

* NOTE: All figures are as of December 31.

TABLE B.1 CONSUMERS' STOCKS BY STATES: ELECTRIC DRYERS, 1946–57
(continued)

Year	Michigan	Wisconsin	Minnesota	Iowa	Missouri	North Dakota
1946	1,778	1,315	889	461	761	109
1947	5,486	4,057	2,742	1,422	2,347	336
1948	14,624	6,832	5,749	3,167	4,746	784
1949	20,966	9,332	9,033	5,595	7,750	1,755
1950	39,273	17,528	18,048	12,412	16,839	3,951
1951	75,458	32,196	31,066	22,821	30,830	7,428
1952	114,558	49,533	46,056	38,297	46,226	14,040
1953	182,406	70,162	65,138	54,138	64,561	18,560
1954	257,019	96,619	89,368	74,578	85,132	24,013
1955	366,217	134,688	120,069	100,100	116,414	29,898
1956	480,228	176,933	154,463	127,395	150,288	36,948
1957	555,862	209,620	180,311	150,282	177,422	42,004

Year	South Dakota	Nebraska	Kansas	Delaware	Maryland and District of Columbia	Virginia
1946	91	245	331	50	576	294
1947	280	755	1,022	155	1,778	906
1948	736	1,919	2,033	361	3,058	1,720
1949	1,546	3,522	3,015	527	4,844	1,942
1950	3,791	7,947	5,963	1,306	10,706	3,080
1951	6,520	13,519	9,025	2,544	19,725	4,601
1952	11,614	21,698	13,570	3,853	29,414	7,010
1953	16,469	30,579	19,042	5,384	39,380	10,251
1954	22,886	41,282	25,853	7,323	52,999	14,055
1955	28,342	56,764	40,712	9,857	74,603	23,652
1956	33,988	70,573	57,066	13,505	99,199	37,451
1957	39,599	82,101	74,709	16,153	114,947	49,573

TABLE B.1 Consumers' Stocks by States: Electric Dryers, 1946–57
(continued)

Year	West Virginia	North Carolina and South Carolina	Georgia	Florida	Kentucky	Tennessee
1946	202	515	513	306	259	468
1947	623	1,589	1,582	945	798	1,444
1948	1,402	2,895	2,262	1,912	1,648	2,348
1949	2,392	3,723	2,702	2,329	2,030	3,203
1950	5,538	5,483	4,564	3,793	3,821	6,161
1951	9,381	7,746	6,638	5,539	6,443	9,058
1952	15,040	10,361	9,231	8,366	9,575	12,631
1953	22,254	14,011	13,088	13,429	14,472	17,683
1954	31,338	18,205	17,523	20,025	20,248	24,776
1955	45,201	27,002	27,245	30,855	32,199	38,597
1956	67,475	38,584	40,141	47,248	47,190	57,487
1957	87,741	49,189	52,089	65,849	62,490	78,672

Year	Alabama	Mississippi	Arkansas	Louisiana	Oklahoma	Texas
1946	260	205	171	337	197	1,027
1947	802	633	527	1,039	608	3,168
1948	1,751	1,277	1,055	2,534	1,628	6,345
1949	2,153	1,455	1,373	3,255	1,946	7,942
1950	3,389	2,040	2,117	5,889	3,033	12,837
1951	4,807	2,754	2,920	8,993	4,575	18,666
1952	6,015	3,065	3,597	11,370	5,844	24,229
1953	8,494	4,203	4,589	15,616	8,336	36,357
1954	10,913	5,307	5,545	20,205	11,858	52,093
1955	17,158	7,577	8,037	30,217	21,248	81,951
1956	26,809	11,002	11,744	47,426	33,821	121,172
1957	37,840	15,239	16,928	67,914	49,256	163,457

TABLE B.1 CONSUMERS' STOCKS BY STATES: ELECTRIC DRYERS, 1946–57
(continued)

Year	Montana	Idaho	Wyoming	Colorado	New Mexico	Arizona
1946	99	113	45	218	61	62
1947	306	348	139	673	189	192
1948	780	1,136	327	1,470	359	416
1949	1,359	2,053	589	2,007	403	500
1950	3,441	4,491	1,250	3,441	555	681
1951	5,918	7,193	2,110	5,438	770	1,038
1952	9,672	11,020	3,374	8,056	1,043	1,574
1953	13,149	14,035	4,698	11,561	1,777	2,571
1954	17,050	17,076	5,919	17,458	3,181	3,453
1955	24,678	23,819	8,370	31,252	6,545	5,282
1956	32,659	32,791	11,025	46,669	10,436	7,682
1957	40,658	39,779	13,099	58,061	14,922	10,599

Year	Utah	Nevada	Washington	Oregon	California
1946	136	38	814	444	1,894
1947	420	118	2,512	1,370	5,843
1948	867	234	6,378	4,583	11,813
1949	1,643	368	10,950	8,481	16,691
1950	3,779	729	27,469	19,967	36,261
1951	6,497	1,260	50,005	36,024	69,421
1952	10,753	2,026	72,538	53,224	115,682
1953	14,516	2,859	98,340	70,302	167,002
1954	18,127	4,109	134,208	88,436	228,478
1955	25,550	5,451	189,960	119,620	339,268
1956	33,417	6,977	241,932	146,827	478,654
1957	39,151	8,200	263,589	158,289	575,116

TABLE B.2 Consumers' Stocks by States: Freezers, 1946–57

Year	Maine	New Hampshire	Vermont	Massa- chusetts	Rhode Island	Con- necticut
1946	1,209	667	417	2,877	730	2,544
1947	4,699	2,593	1,620	11,180	2,836	9,885
1948	8,666	4,782	2,988	20,619	5,230	18,230
1949	11,459	6,243	3,949	25,681	6,351	22,562
1950	16,200	9,006	5,941	38,742	8,842	31,766
1951	20,993	11,750	7,914	53,287	11,881	42,255
1952	24,937	13,768	9,524	67,698	13,890	50,793
1953	28,735	16,335	11,102	86,834	16,335	61,823
1954	32,051	17,592	12,359	95,369	17,474	69,351
1955	36,195	18,910	13,560	102,545	18,349	79,892
1956	39,474	19,559	14,954	109,103	18,697	86,032
1957	43,925	20,565	16,552	116,861	19,350	92,110

Year	New York	New Jersey	Pennsyl- vania	Ohio	Indiana	Illinois
1946	11,926	3,836	13,073	13,031	8,423	12,572
1947	46,344	14,907	20,801	50,638	32,733	48,855
1948	85,469	27,492	93,688	93,388	60,367	90,100
1949	106,255	35,563	121,567	118,214	79,778	120,178
1950	153,594	51,711	171,973	171,542	110,141	169,751
1951	210,752	69,659	229,085	228,750	141,844	229,864
1952	283,318	100,579	286,260	284,254	170,352	275,600
1953	346,639	123,994	344,155	352,342	207,446	327,005
1954	391,670	138,485	394,297	411,648	239,067	366,586
1955	430,772	154,079	453,346	469,355	271,646	405,864
1956	463,449	166,774	493,646	510,316	300,867	448,849
1957	502,120	184,172	533,610	547,506	324,410	485,798

TABLE B.2 CONSUMERS' STOCKS BY STATES: FREEZERS, 1946–57

(continued)

Year	Michigan	Wisconsin	Minnesota	Iowa	Missouri	North Dakota
1946	7,777	6,484	5,796	5,441	6,297	2,231
1947	30,221	25,197	22,253	21,145	24,469	8,670
1948	55,734	46,469	41,438	38,997	45,126	15,989
1949	70,672	59,148	55,575	55,888	58,731	21,880
1950	102,338	81,130	78,245	81,068	88,070	30,851
1951	137,281	110,679	105,674	112,808	122,925	44,505
1952	176,068	133,124	129,123	139,675	158,708	54,883
1953	214,685	156,311	151,534	168,996	196,218	63,994
1954	244,286	175,793	173,396	194,009	230,150	73,432
1955	275,748	196,977	199,228	220,496	265,513	83,985
1956	305,414	214,025	220,228	236,862	298,994	89,609
1957	338,075	233,267	238,463	254,426	328,300	95,909

Year	South Dakota	Nebraska	Kansas	Delaware	Maryland and District of Columbia	Virginia
1946	1,397	2,857	2,377	354	4,232	2,690
1947	5,429	11,101	9,237	1,377	16,446	10,452
1948	10,012	20,472	17,035	2,540	30,331	19,276
1949	15,843	28,020	24,819	3,604	39,988	26,315
1950	24,809	45,326	36,312	5,601	58,748	39,394
1951	38,233	69,064	53,238	8,827	81,874	54,393
1952	48,074	88,735	70,190	10,895	106,804	71,072
1953	57,389	114,175	87,454	13,432	126,239	88,365
1954	68,273	133,278	102,023	15,372	148,124	106,400
1955	79,871	150,285	116,492	17,642	174,646	126,396
1956	83,901	158,137	127,295	19,429	196,187	146,262
1957	88,582	167,034	136,104	21,248	218,822	165,572

TABLE B.2 Consumers' Stocks by States: Freezers, 1946–57

(continued)

Year	West Virginia	North Carolina and South Carolina	Georgia	Florida	Kentucky	Tennessee
1946	2,794	6,546	2,981	3,398	2,460	3,857
1947	10,857	25,439	11,585	13,206	9,560	14,989
1948	20,023	46,916	21,366	24,355	17,631	27,643
1949	25,428	63,027	30,478	32,661	23,738	37,575
1950	34,518	92,518	47,418	47,968	33,746	54,251
1951	43,610	125,976	66,999	62,605	45,698	73,019
1952	53,114	166,190	90,676	78,611	59,282	92,754
1953	65,238	203,745	115,666	97,620	77,576	115,324
1954	78,141	245,597	141,512	119,632	96,451	140,840
1955	92,244	300,407	180,626	146,886	115,278	173,147
1956	101,960	348,491	213,149	170,969	133,491	204,672
1957	110,590	393,092	242,009	192,246	150,825	230,720

Year	Alabama	Mississippi	Arkansas	Louisiana	Oklahoma	Texas
1946	2,523	2,106	2,627	5,150	3,232	16,580
1947	9,804	8,183	10,209	20,013	12,559	64,430
1948	18,081	15,091	18,828	36,908	23,161	118,824
1949	23,657	20,803	26,160	49,147	29,955	152,132
1950	36,311	32,350	37,567	74,180	40,770	215,536
1951	49,385	43,450	49,689	96,175	55,134	284,163
1952	64,637	58,098	62,799	119,728	73,290	351,512
1953	81,971	74,799	76,643	144,026	93,705	415,687
1954	99,690	91,639	91,023	170,469	106,725	469,600
1955	128,213	114,361	108,430	200,095	117,008	528,169
1956	150,811	132,166	121,429	226,964	126,362	584,054
1957	171,347	146,140	131,441	251,667	133,997	631,652

TABLE B.2 Consumers' Stocks by States: Freezers, 1946–57
(continued)

Year	Montana	Idaho	Wyoming	Colorado	New Mexico	Arizona
1946	1,564	1,460	521	2,627	751	1,334
1947	6,077	5,672	2,025	10,208	2,918	5,185
1948	11,207	10,460	3,735	18,826	5,381	9,563
1949	15,541	14,422	5,450	25,537	7,312	11,866
1950	22,810	21,171	8,050	37,651	11,569	17,478
1951	32,894	26,839	11,652	50,909	15,947	21,728
1952	41,142	33,314	16,042	65,249	21,082	30,795
1953	49,577	37,891	19,168	80,563	26,357	35,087
1954	57,002	42,244	21,707	93,246	32,015	37,790
1955	63,625	47,445	24,019	105,219	37,482	40,425
1956	68,600	52,645	25,647	114,817	44,163	45,676
1957	72,535	58,393	27,124	123,829	49,704	52,417

Year	Utah	Nevada	Washington	Oregon	California
1946	1,562	542	3,836	3,607	17,805
1947	6,075	2,106	14,908	14,016	69,191
1948	11,205	3,884	27,494	25,849	127,604
1949	15,014	4,881	34,418	33,609	153,243
1950	21,134	6,595	50,124	48,719	212,900
1951	30,805	9,159	63,528	63,103	273,927
1952	45,539	12,428	80,134	80,418	412,534
1953	51,350	14,395	95,571	95,596	446,175
1954	56,136	15,794	107,610	108,098	467,941
1955	60,147	17,366	122,264	122,524	500,762
1956	63,835	18,617	144,792	133,382	547,697
1957	68,205	19,806	165,456	144,536	600,523

TABLE B.3 Consumers' Stocks by States: Ironing Machines, 1944–57

Year	Maine	New Hampshire	Vermont	Massa-chusetts	Rhode Island	Con-necticut
1944	11,393	9,655	5,406	65,268	10,042	46,151
1945	11,352	9,620	5,386	65,031	10,006	45,984
1946	11,946	9,903	5,616	68,028	10,667	46,686
1947	13,377	10,601	6,105	77,346	12,552	73,001
1948	15,841	11,183	6,732	88,188	14,613	79,049
1949	16,792	11,731	7,222	96,145	15,765	82,451
1950	17,946	12,597	7,735	106,504	17,559	87,229
1951	18,827	13,239	8,175	115,298	19,444	92,040
1952	19,406	13,645	8,383	119,609	20,213	91,898
1953	19,968	14,027	8,623	122,800	20,801	92,016
1954	20,185	14,307	8,750	125,282	21,195	91,725
1955	20,418	14,498	8,851	126,611	21,511	90,717
1956	20,580	14,674	8,949	127,524	21,627	89,886
1957	20,694	14,793	8,959	127,953	21,680	88,999

Year	New York	New Jersey	Pennsyl-vania	Ohio	Indiana	Illinois
1944	190,010	72,027	196,920	186,920	56,579	156,798
1945	189,321	71,766	195,862	186,242	56,374	156,230
1946	200,148	74,857	207,810	201,727	63,664	175,022
1947	224,403	84,280	234,299	236,103	76,088	197,672
1948	262,080	91,582	271,035	268,404	88,453	225,627
1949	284,913	98,040	291,879	290,286	95,603	244,684
1950	313,167	107,180	317,118	313,537	104,069	265,305
1951	337,948	116,996	339,820	334,283	116,980	280,810
1952	354,155	123,170	355,472	350,946	122,001	292,272
1953	367,602	128,317	369,045	365,481	126,306	300,518
1954	375,585	131,367	376,140	373,911	128,475	305,846
1955	380,468	131,606	383,540	382,880	130,095	305,760
1956	381,910	133,185	388,365	387,856	131,390	306,046
1957	382,771	134,119	391,577	390,846	132,026	305,119

TABLE B.3 Consumers' Stocks by States: Ironing Machines, 1944–57
(continued)

Year	Michigan	Wisconsin	Minnesota	Iowa	Missouri	North Dakota
1944	132,080	55,034	48,467	28,772	49,434	4,673
1945	131,601	54,835	48,291	28,668	49,255	4,656
1946	141,091	60,181	51,477	30,950	52,940	5,142
1947	161,612	67,789	59,015	40,129	62,363	6,468
1948	191,762	77,376	70,439	47,342	75,714	8,663
1949	209,521	83,344	77,762	53,627	84,161	10,306
1950	228,763	89,117	83,952	60,330	95,289	11,428
1951	251,123	92,681	87,544	65,458	100,306	12,912
1952	273,423	93,543	92,261	68,413	108,772	14,211
1953	294,885	95,981	95,975	71,311	115,270	14,914
1954	304,815	96,332	97,945	72,608	118,448	15,328
1955	319,072	96,337	100,080	73,720	121,969	15,736
1956	326,283	95,881	101,760	73,985	124,017	15,943
1957	331,532	95,053	102,468	73,811	125,465	16,327

Year	South Dakota	Nebraska	Kansas	Delaware	Maryland and District of Columbia	Virginia
1944	4,596	19,117	15,448	4,055	33,793	11,007
1945	4,579	19,048	15,392	4,040	33,671	10,967
1946	5,065	20,236	16,715	4,175	35,410	11,980
1947	5,972	24,215	19,437	4,489	41,887	15,854
1948	8,346	28,785	24,544	5,251	50,220	20,244
1949	9,989	32,822	27,975	5,655	58,091	22,954
1950	11,560	36,959	32,016	6,360	65,499	25,648
1951	12,875	40,170	35,491	7,144	73,823	27,005
1952	13,942	42,762	37,845	7,862	80,586	28,660
1953	14,710	44,804	39,577	8,417	84,504	29,958
1954	15,309	45,809	40,660	8,639	86,928	30,499
1955	15,844	46,716	41,926	8,881	89,071	30,856
1956	16,100	47,070	43,356	8,977	90,170	31,175
1957	16,274	47,438	44,263	9,070	90,794	31,345

TABLE B.3 Consumers' Stocks by States: Ironing Machines, 1944–57
(continued)

Year	West Virginia	North Carolina and South Carolina	Georgia	Florida	Kentucky	Tennessee
1944	22,593	10,317	11,393	10,427	13,324	14,483
1945	22,511	8,197	11,352	10,389	13,276	14,431
1946	24,185	11,749	11,919	11,145	14,329	14,469
1947	28,478	16,568	15,619	15,787	17,156	22,262
1948	34,884	24,907	22,384	21,477	21,501	29,296
1949	38,459	29,145	25,930	24,475	23,577	32,698
1950	42,628	33,506	30,035	29,318	25,822	36,482
1951	45,604	36,044	32,176	32,254	27,404	38,680
1952	47,464	37,698	34,000	33,822	28,198	39,928
1953	48,849	38,866	35,931	34,918	28,620	40,676
1954	49,511	39,341	36,743	35,398	28,919	40,979
1955	50,066	39,759	37,334	35,701	29,201	41,163
1956	50,390	39,906	37,613	35,874	29,474	41,164
1957	50,762	39,996	37,692	35,941	29,491	40,842

Year	Alabama	Mississippi	Arkansas	Louisiana	Oklahoma	Texas
1944	7,337	2,124	3,475	7,337	12,938	29,352
1945	7,310	2,116	3,462	7,310	12,891	29,246
1946	8,080	2,359	4,218	8,417	14,147	32,364
1947	10,174	4,244	6,103	11,314	17,672	42,624
1948	13,713	5,857	8,343	16,780	23,317	62,291
1949	15,327	7,673	10,102	20,268	26,748	76,792
1950	17,187	8,924	11,962	23,828	31,206	94,302
1951	18,181	9,693	12,989	25,827	34,459	103,423
1952	18,633	10,171	13,499	26,830	36,825	110,554
1953	19,020	10,464	13,836	27,477	38,542	115,580
1954	19,295	10,536	13,992	28,061	39,514	118,829
1955	19,454	10,563	14,049	28,401	40,572	122,736
1956	19,599	10,574	14,044	28,606	41,475	124,975
1957	19,683	10,549	14,027	28,730	41,958	125,601

TABLE B.3 Consumers' Stocks by States: Ironing Machines, 1944–57
(continued)

Year	Montana	Idaho	Wyoming	Colorado	New Mexico	Arizona
1944	8,496	6,952	4,055	16,799	1,931	6,180
1945	8,465	6,927	4,040	16,738	1,924	6,158
1946	8,802	7,062	4,135	17,723	2,167	6,563
1947	9,884	7,655	4,414	19,817	2,935	7,296
1948	13,020	9,716	5,086	25,686	3,831	9,491
1949	15,096	11,936	5,749	28,367	5,186	10,588
1950	16,988	13,764	6,454	32,536	7,046	12,290
1951	18,631	15,002	7,088	33,125	8,144	13,593
1952	19,720	15,672	7,429	35,160	8,944	14,474
1953	20,736	16,348	7,777	37,021	9,603	14,990
1954	21,350	16,824	7,900	38,256	9,988	15,335
1955	22,140	18,315	7,971	39,059	10,394	15,615
1956	22,497	20,194	8,121	40,755	10,813	16,909
1957	24,102	21,575	8,254	41,669	10,984	18,551

Year	Utah	Nevada	Washington	Oregon	California
1944	11,200	2,124	50,592	26,841	237,513
1945	11,160	2,116	50,408	26,744	236,652
1946	11,903	2,197	52,473	27,851	247,007
1947	13,683	2,651	60,535	32,318	283,792
1948	18,028	3,861	75,050	43,787	332,221
1949	20,565	4,437	83,065	47,708	368,691
1950	23,964	5,208	90,730	53,320	400,633
1951	26,147	5,570	94,846	57,483	428,459
1952	28,241	5,792	97,898	59,812	445,793
1953	29,464	5,895	100,797	61,723	458,124
1954	30,340	6,014	102,984	62,919	464,900
1955	32,707	6,384	104,294	64,090	469,870
1956	35,253	6,942	105,703	65,198	475,176
1957	36,589	7,285	106,893	66,326	478,930

TABLE B.4 Consumers' Stocks by States: Electric Ranges, 1944–57

Year	Maine	New Hampshire	Vermont	Massa-chusetts	Rhode Island	Con-necticut
1944	33,815	26,500	14,819	94,482	17,840	62,888
1945	33,692	26,204	14,764	94,136	17,775	62,658
1946	37,142	28,002	16,368	104,488	20,837	70,483
1947	42,400	32,040	18,578	120,490	25,333	82,523
1948	49,859	36,872	21,204	139,293	30,901	95,864
1949	56,085	40,763	23,018	159,532	35,745	108,058
1950	66,944	47,158	25,694	201,783	45,862	131,116
1951	72,892	51,285	27,778	242,283	56,348	156,438
1952	77,418	53,920	29,472	274,927	64,458	171,926
1953	83,584	58,208	31,875	316,657	76,659	195,913
1954	88,790	61,277	33,226	348,581	87,791	214,490
1955	92,397	63,861	33,569	372,379	98,038	235,084
1956	100,939	70,097	37,232	421,710	107,632	266,170
1957	92,150	63,603	32,663	455,657	109,537	282,581

Year	New York	New Jersey	Pennsyl-vania	Ohio	Indiana	Illinois
1944	167,161	51,996	264,316	271,442	142,037	189,098
1945	166,550	51,806	263,349	270,449	141,517	188,406
1946	190,218	59,290	295,717	308,454	159,256	213,532
1947	226,032	74,683	351,038	366,214	187,374	255,061
1948	274,464	89,286	425,524	431,976	228,032	304,332
1949	317,800	102,346	482,777	476,760	257,522	335,888
1950	394,563	128,829	580,657	559,011	301,101	396,574
1951	470,655	150,504	664,211	622,416	333,901	433,217
1952	515,574	161,191	723,513	669,975	355,131	452,536
1953	576,227	178,250	802,977	737,044	387,140	484,963
1954	622,272	197,424	854,796	778,827	405,738	499,907
1955	675,899	222,265	886,084	810,673	414,264	494,397
1956	758,284	251,903	979,009	898,175	453,573	538,350
1957	823,877	276,444	1,037,844	933,148	474,482	558,503

TABLE B.4 Consumers' Stocks by States: Electric Ranges, 1944–57
(continued)

Year	Michigan	Wisconsin	Minnesota	Iowa	Missouri	North Dakota
1944	312,215	133,205	118,364	58,091	91,767	21,643
1945	311,074	132,717	117,931	57,879	91,432	21,563
1946	347,281	145,207	132,511	69,057	107,713	24,042
1947	393,915	166,238	151,789	85,059	134,154	27,776
1948	441,179	193,445	178,052	107,332	163,466	35,657
1949	476,524	214,542	194,129	124,546	185,519	42,492
1950	542,550	249,345	218,962	148,939	222,111	51,417
1951	592,535	270,488	231,577	164,316	246,683	58,840
1952	618,331	285,918	240,431	173,796	262,849	64,676
1953	666,046	309,597	255,375	186,006	281,186	70,695
1954	705,028	324,897	262,751	192,117	289,678	74,474
1955	748,931	338,213	268,964	200,575	309,918	79,857
1956	828,480	373,476	297,065	218,001	340,506	85,799
1957	759,242	365,281	282,921	232,606	362,451	92,252

Year	South Dakota	Nebraska	Kansas	Delaware, Maryland and District of Columbia	Virginia
1944	21,608	22,480	31,523	63,688	73,282
1945	21,529	22,398	31,407	63,275	73,014
1946	23,570	27,792	36,170	74,831	82,783
1947	27,304	36,174	42,952	92,562	98,175
1948	34,764	53,091	54,194	111,427	122,970
1949	40,732	64,549	61,891	123,089	145,983
1950	49,658	83,346	76,173	155,376	184,663
1951	55,563	97,639	85,833	198,679	215,115
1952	59,097	108,156	91,651	225,059	244,131
1953	63,714	120,889	98,901	256,529	274,842
1954	66,208	132,028	106,170	287,850	297,684
1955	69,034	144,390	119,003	320,023	318,948
1956	73,821	156,434	135,658	349,519	356,756
1957	77,809	165,058	149,072	381,668	383,986

TABLE B.4 Consumers' Stocks by States: Electric Ranges, 1944–57
(continued)

Year	West Virginia	North Carolina and South Carolina	Georgia	Florida	Kentucky	Tennessee
1944	30,156	151,931	93,412	112,874	23,704	120,195
1945	30,046	151,376	93,070	112,461	23,617	119,756
1946	36,412	169,452	103,470	126,701	29,400	136,912
1947	47,232	199,194	123,206	148,647	36,867	164,954
1948	65,409	257,822	159,034	182,896	53,469	214,021
1949	82,023	324,625	192,171	212,999	70,950	265,851
1950	108,804	436,367	246,773	277,602	97,288	352,594
1951	128,748	518,241	288,217	326,545	119,377	405,923
1952	145,292	597,008	327,810	365,369	140,878	451,581
1953	165,586	684,827	365,458	413,560	167,785	501,870
1954	181,114	738,786	390,412	463,160	186,303	530,298
1955	199,085	799,846	416,514	533,431	207,863	564,506
1956	217,082	907,868	464,029	626,550	233,829	619,581
1957	232,378	982,992	501,593	716,222	258,996	661,889

Year	Alabama	Mississippi	Arkansas	Louisiana	Oklahoma	Texas
1944	65,430	15,885	8,867	7,623	7,180	60,644
1945	65,191	15,826	8,834	7,596	7,154	60,422
1946	73,356	19,471	11,167	9,783	9,390	72,086
1947	87,986	24,653	15,511	12,983	12,971	89,764
1948	111,941	32,323	21,920	16,345	19,599	114,980
1949	139,111	41,063	28,757	19,373	25,051	134,356
1950	181,963	54,453	36,790	24,878	33,626	173,933
1951	209,055	62,706	43,444	28,768	39,451	201,747
1952	233,745	71,910	49,912	32,531	44,759	222,788
1953	260,312	82,495	56,013	37,198	51,368	247,878
1954	281,755	91,066	60,259	42,379	58,276	273,330
1955	314,369	100,272	65,018	49,513	66,313	322,827
1956	352,243	111,110	71,733	59,148	77,474	375,360
1957	384,487	120,774	78,111	69,578	87,590	419,711

TABLE B.4 CONSUMERS' STOCKS BY STATES: ELECTRIC RANGES, 1944–57
(continued)

Year	Montana	Idaho	Wyoming	Colorado	New Mexico	Arizona
1944	24,451	42,115	4,620	22,265	3,482	7,338
1945	24,361	41,962	4,603	22,183	3,469	7,311
1946	27,277	47,259	5,575	26,411	4,247	8,672
1947	32,077	53,584	6,794	32,888	5,009	11,187
1948	39,010	67,873	8,895	42,869	6,480	14,234
1949	44,545	78,080	10,366	50,482	7,950	16,223
1950	53,469	93,847	13,192	62,830	11,224	19,645
1951	59,400	102,634	15,522	72,059	14,520	22,018
1952	64,650	109,889	17,071	78,178	17,355	24,030
1953	71,247	118,387	19,110	86,347	21,102	26,193
1954	76,509	124,480	20,785	95,438	24,779	28,212
1955	80,806	130,348	22,809	111,658	29,323	30,882
1956	89,616	140,157	25,098	128,930	34,983	36,334
1957	91,860	132,861	32,652	143,792	39,834	44,873

Year	Utah	Nevada	Washington	Oregon	California
1944	41,368	9,240	174,865	111,135	131,160
1945	41,217	9,206	174,226	110,728	130,680
1946	47,292	10,615	197,165	126,183	153,960
1947	55,674	12,825	232,903	152,396	191,831
1948	66,810	15,662	282,595	189,904	233,014
1949	74,679	18,344	319,925	216,455	262,243
1950	88,512	22,361	374,637	257,659	312,371
1951	99,770	25,690	416,559	287,337	363,045
1952	109,177	28,607	446,806	310,220	386,393
1953	118,663	33,656	487,310	334,257	421,790
1954	125,237	37,844	516,802	343,463	463,340
1955	131,762	41,527	532,404	362,515	534,659
1956	143,532	44,727	577,542	392,924	636,517
1957	144,548	47,129	592,462	410,926	722,223

TABLE B.5 Consumers' Stocks by States: Electric Refrigerators, 1944–57

Year	Maine	New Hampshire	Vermont	Massachusetts	Rhode Island	Connecticut
1944	89,064	65,314	43,543	779,804	112,814	344,381
1945	88,740	65,077	43,385	776,967	112,403	343,128
1946	97,512	70,753	46,825	832,007	126,679	313,916
1947	108,354	78,259	50,787	896,642	144,401	410,612
1948	129,697	92,717	58,705	999,226	174,694	464,313
1949	153,400	106,200	67,850	1,017,750	194,700	480,850
1950	179,750	121,075	75,925	1,140,000	215,675	527,175
1951	189,054	125,593	78,526	1,164,011	234,903	547,712
1952	201,087	132,334	81,721	1,213,725	253,795	571,680
1953	207,942	135,490	82,347	1,213,815	265,794	589,929
1954	218,628	141,235	82,506	1,266,084	273,473	621,881
1955	228,702	147,484	84,392	1,302,839	296,493	653,455
1956	238,892	153,331	88,640	1,364,608	312,137	680,831
1957	248,187	158,544	92,210	1,415,022	324,998	704,584

Year	New York	New Jersey	Pennsylvania	Ohio	Indiana	Illinois
1944	2,574,939	843,139	1,775,343	1,276,584	532,405	1,502,213
1945	2,565,571	840,072	1,768,885	1,271,900	530,468	1,496,748
1946	2,760,275	904,400	1,911,473	1,397,500	577,596	1,612,676
1947	2,980,034	989,260	2,072,226	1,534,902	640,354	1,746,324
1948	3,328,061	1,112,153	2,319,046	1,735,200	739,839	1,959,753
1949	3,312,850	1,147,550	2,301,000	1,846,700	843,700	1,979,450
1950	3,701,300	1,281,425	2,569,600	2,045,175	949,100	2,182,175
1951	3,934,823	1,354,438	2,641,959	2,122,491	983,360	2,239,653
1952	4,175,309	1,433,244	2,753,480	2,232,696	1,040,770	2,324,717
1953	4,380,831	1,463,832	2,858,346	2,277,135	1,085,766	2,385,473
1954	4,619,598	1,514,056	2,928,769	2,411,617	1,159,204	2,476,558
1955	4,790,247	1,596,256	2,980,611	2,541,269	1,236,535	2,532,163
1956	5,021,922	1,676,406	3,069,879	2,666,759	1,308,103	2,619,949
1957	5,214,494	1,744,675	3,129,267	2,752,776	1,367,547	2,700,691

TABLE B.5 Consumers' Stocks by States: Electric Refrigerators, 1944–57　　*(continued)*

Year	Michigan	Wisconsin	Minnesota	Iowa	Missouri	North Dakota
1944	940,120	397,819	423,549	326,568	579,905	37,605
1945	936,700	396,372	422,008	325,380	577,795	37,468
1946	1,020,120	433,008	456,924	355,308	653,243	42,800
1947	1,122,494	480,338	500,084	393,464	708,009	50,097
1948	1,276,025	557,448	575,472	460,247	818,510	63,178
1949	1,416,000	637,200	651,950	539,850	843,700	82,600
1950	1,567,725	720,500	731,850	618,050	990,750	102,150
1951	1,624,684	755,518	756,841	642,690	1,052,427	115,709
1952	1,711,774	787,168	783,661	668,534	1,129,459	125,390
1953	1,760,213	807,411	798,443	686,140	1,196,739	130,373
1954	1,872,834	839,353	815,760	710,502	1,261,971	137,427
1955	2,007,540	869,729	823,106	728,087	1,308,309	146,407
1956	2,139,333	903,367	839,667	740,976	1,353,416	152,313
1957	2,237,194	931,948	848,998	754,258	1,384,734	158,343

Year	South Dakota	Nebraska	Kansas	Delaware	Maryland and District of Columbia	Virginia
1944	47,501	160,315	213,754	45,522	459,174	312,714
1945	47,328	159,732	212,977	45,357	457,503	311,577
1946	53,176	175,384	228,629	48,797	505,835	336,173
1947	60,682	196,651	250,521	53,384	650,254	367,239
1948	75,829	231,419	285,633	59,925	653,543	420,940
1949	97,350	253,700	336,300	70,800	581,150(a)	492,650
1950	116,900	299,600	384,750	80,150	692,075	564,900
1951	127,567	318,045	402,645	87,480	748,435	599,846
1952	136,933	336,424	428,380	93,297	801,798	650,710
1953	143,467	351,261	434,029	96,700	844,442	677,374
1954	150,702	368,022	447,708	103,171	931,301	714,052
1955	156,446	379,811	464,893	110,568	1,038,102	749,757
1956	158,651	391,141	493,862	115,812	1,126,623	801,640
1957	162,067	399,645	516,709	121,363	1,201,483	837,420

(a) Figure from *Electrical Merchandising*, possibly a misprint for 681,150.

TABLE B.5 Consumers' Stocks by States: Electric Refrigerators,
1944–57   *(continued)*

Year	West Virginia	North Carolina and South Carolina	Georgia	Florida	Kentucky	Tennessee
1944	215,733	504,795	306,776	277,088	259,275	314,693
1945	214,948	502,858	305,660	276,080	258,332	313,548
1946	237,136	546,202	331,460	301,708	280,692	343,992
1947	263,189	596,867	367,114	335,694	305,295	382,147
1948	306,916	692,910	435,618	402,477	351,767	456,503
1949	345,150	852,550	528,050	483,800	433,650	581,150
1950	405,925	1,033,175	627,925	586,650	510,575	706,100
1951	426,732	1,102,989	671,530	661,549	541,568	749,786
1952	457,874	1,202,198	737,143	753,015	584,979	812,884
1953	487,091	1,283,054	786,590	831,617	609,694	873,528
1954	505,968	1,341,200	839,723	905,787	643,895	917,655
1955	523,182	1,398,264	895,995	991,186	672,158	952,819
1956	540,064	1,464,882	951,642	1,110,458	708,192	983,731
1957	550,471	1,504,024	997,184	1,237,322	736,007	1,002,626

Year	Alabama	Mississippi	Arkansas	Louisiana	Oklahoma	Texas
1944	219,691	104,898	122,710	211,774	203,858	777,826
1945	218,892	104,517	122,263	211,003	203,117	774,997
1946	236,608	115,353	135,163	230,267	219,629	846,377
1947	260,377	129,323	151,426	255,079	242,564	949,376
1948	308,226	157,207	184,129	304,305	285,594	1,123,906
1949	386,450	212,400	259,600	392,350	356,950	1,392,400
1950	471,025	268,925	329,300	476,925	434,300	1,680,125
1951	503,720	296,000	356,191	522,870	463,535	1,776,586
1952	551,836	334,168	392,006	572,802	503,545	1,908,706
1953	590,270	358,656	422,137	606,903	529,038	2,020,581
1954	626,925	371,608	443,754	637,129	560,996	2,127,315
1955	664,123	395,511	461,834	659,211	587,132	2,230,537
1956	701,959	422,729	480,719	711,695	622,279	2,357,103
1957	733,080	447,365	492,219	766,093	645,522	2,456,516

TABLE B.5 Consumers' Stocks by States: Electric Refrigerators,
1944–57   *(continued)*

Year	Montana	Idaho	Wyoming	Colorado	New Mexico	Arizona
1944	65,313	75,210	25,730	140,523	35,626	63,334
1945	65,075	74,937	25,637	140,011	35,497	63,103
1946	70,923	81,645	28,045	156,523	39,109	69,295
1947	78,012	89,359	30,964	175,496	43,487	78,261
1948	90,405	103,129	35,439	206,822	53,126	97,538
1949	106,200	118,000	41,300	247,800	67,850	118,000
1950	119,375	131,600	47,250	292,850	84,000	140,100
1951	123,212	133,070	50,163	311,305	91,473	149,713
1952	129,189	136,823	53,016	332,454	100,695	165,731
1953	130,758	134,698	55,052	351,822	109,326	181,193
1954	137,632	137,656	57,712	372,639	116,865	196,326
1955	144,415	142,454	59,406	393,325	123,789	210,315
1956	150,846	148,094	61,300	414,459	134,506	226,306
1957	154,503	151,955	62,705	429,335	141,742	241,853

Year	Utah	Nevada	Washington	Oregon	California
1944	98,960	21,771	310,734	184,066	1,367,627
1945	98,600	21,692	309,604	183,397	1,362,651
1946	108,060	24,616	342,456	206,445	1,485,287
1947	119,528	28,161	379,360	234,384	1,634,156
1948	137,084	34,701	442,356	277,414	1,888,205
1949	144,550	32,450	489,700	318,600	2,135,800
1950	163,675	38,400	541,125	363,225	2,439,675
1951	167,355	41,816	554,016	377,902	2,578,359
1952	174,222	44,852	574,885	396,913	2,761,870
1953	180,288	49,400	590,567	412,931	2,929,273
1954	185,515	55,681	610,549	427,371	3,113,641
1955	188,185	61,859	624,739	441,174	3,304,985
1956	195,159	66,520	642,514	452,725	3,533,939
1957	199,036	70,090	659,248	460,591	3,753,284

TABLE B.6 Consumers' Stocks by States: Washing Machines, 1944–57

Year	Maine	New Hampshire	Vermont	Massachusetts	Rhode Island	Connecticut
1944	114,028	58,742	55,286	608,151	91,568	279,888
1945	113,632	58,537	55,094	606,037	91,250	278,923
1946	124,243	64,073	58,951	655,319	99,099	299,422
1947	136,648	69,064	64,134	725,112	110,847	327,779
1948	152,040	74,432	70,627	805,728	124,629	365,687
1949	161,916	78,676	73,456	857,123	133,753	387,769
1950	172,085	85,457	77,329	930,986	148,528	419,735
1951	176,690	89,861	78,421	998,742	159,916	436,134
1952	193,166	95,920	80,374	1,066,011	172,812	461,092
1953	196,233	99,368	80,192	1,128,784	185,755	497,349
1954	193,754	104,544	74,528	1,194,562	203,783	538,051
1955	202,359	110,693	79,377	1,267,412	211,484	581,239
1956	209,178	116,887	81,124	1,319,088	215,375	613,978
1957	211,565	120,694	79,397	1,373,698	231,280	640,419

Year	New York	New Jersey	Pennsylvania	Ohio	Indiana	Illinois
1944	1,268,134	504,489	1,876,285	1,425,355	620,245	1,406,350
1945	1,263,725	502,735	1,869,764	1,420,400	618,090	1,401,461
1946	1,394,763	542,330	2,005,325	1,538,036	669,361	1,523,341
1947	1,584,162	603,388	2,163,112	1,678,683	728,443	1,659,906
1948	1,806,035	669,899	2,400,638	1,867,502	809,355	1,837,822
1949	1,936,409	720,745	2,554,427	1,977,143	862,341	1,934,559
1950	2,149,799	799,949	2,745,967	2,120,248	925,298	2,060,374
1951	2,383,516	878,334	2,904,981	2,252,494	960,487	2,150,364
1952	2,668,056	942,826	3,036,395	2,327,187	1,004,157	2,230,875
1953	2,802,306	1,002,900	3,128,422	2,460,953	1,035,911	2,321,289
1954	3,019,552	1,087,033	3,182,033	2,521,860	1,080,982	2,376,859
1955	3,191,185	1,177,186	3,220,365	2,654,233	1,141,602	2,448,003
1956	3,397,180	1,280,867	3,438,038	2,756,287	1,189,728	2,539,514
1957	3,724,227	1,345,274	3,322,534	2,691,062	1,205,937	2,457,498

TABLE B.6 Consumers' Stocks by States: Washing Machines, 1944-57
(continued)

Year	Michigan	Wisconsin	Minnesota	Iowa	Missouri	North Dakota
1944	1,031,439	551,137	552,865	461,297	689,353	91,568
1945	1,027,853	549,221	550,943	459,693	686,957	91,250
1946	1,107,062	598,906	592,105	499,095	744,230	99,251
1947	1,202,070	651,769	641,307	544,465	818,253	107,554
1948	1,330,797	714,736	702,527	597,940	930,276	119,899
1949	1,411,036	752,356	733,439	614,078	989,742	127,430
1950	1,510,797	797,385	770,472	672,837	1,063,839	134,450
1951	1,577,410	827,411	789,390	697,893	1,108,913	140,476
1952	1,641,462	854,410	808,495	711,683	1,162,964	142,184
1953	1,661,275	873,508	815,227	719,469	1,203,759	144,418
1954	1,762,612	884,224	823,627	728,845	1,252,593	145,907
1955	1,875,742	907,385	827,672	732,167	1,295,476	145,021
1956	1,949,292	933,200	834,851	735,517	1,319,512	144,803
1957	1,979,215	899,335	774,703	704,591	1,297,255	147,304

Year	South Dakota	Nebraska	Kansas	Delaware	Maryland and District of Columbia	Virginia
1944	100,207	219,418	252,245	43,193	329,990	193,248
1945	99,859	218,655	251,368	43,042	328,843	192,830
1946	108,477	237,889	272,002	46,279	359,354	215,237
1947	118,031	261,259	290,633	50,019	404,334	247,478
1948	131,250	291,810	335,349	55,038	470,170	301,088
1949	139,866	309,649	354,538	59,229	512,388	332,303
1950	148,339	331,442	378,992	64,800	572,458	370,088
1951	153,996	342,179	395,550	69,592	631,393	400,863
1952	161,356	352,724	410,006	75,435	696,567	445,787
1953	166,100	359,303	413,525	76,215	751,082	482,386
1954	170,858	369,858	420,876	86,750	823,410	521,489
1955	169,624	380,449	445,893	94,014	819,914	574,656
1956	166,513	386,931	465,992	99,396	920,267	639,184
1957	163,744	381,947	468,703	100,899	987,908	711,743

TABLE B.6 Consumers' Stocks by States: Washing Machines, 1944–57
(continued)

Year	West Virginia	North Carolina and South Carolina	Georgia	Florida	Kentucky	Tennessee
1944	281,616	165,859	86,385	93,297	229,784	222,874
1945	280,637	165,283	86,085	92,973	228,986	222,099
1946	300,233	190,556	104,890	110,720	250,209	250,013
1947	323,323	236,933	142,383	138,498	276,846	299,547
1948	375,763	324,736	206,475	185,463	335,404	388,134
1949	406,656	389,740	249,901	219,697	368,820	441,719
1950	443,468	497,731	349,803	283,001	403,937	504,218
1951	469,693	590,656	408,367	338,124	424,952	533,263
1952	491,397	699,942	485,231	410,684	453,935	584,911
1953	495,231	808,757	558,252	489,600	482,423	658,945
1954	521,136	919,815	639,589	577,330	506,691	743,901
1955	528,488	1,059,495	736,034	680,040	533,051	829,907
1956	536,127	1,178,087	825,893	783,115	561,145	902,177
1957	555,464	1,308,596	914,834	912,090	616,171	976,024

Year	Alabama	Mississippi	Arkansas	Louisiana	Oklahoma	Texas
1944	82,930	20,732	65,653	150,310	236,694	430,199
1945	82,642	20,660	65,425	149,787	235,871	428,704
1946	94,746	27,835	75,076	167,587	256,035	481,931
1947	115,805	40,048	88,600	198,518	284,305	570,022
1948	154,991	56,158	115,427	250,535	320,639	720,567
1949	185,102	75,282	138,227	291,447	338,382	815,992
1950	225,078	124,519	163,907	341,596	365,504	957,475
1951	279,011	152,298	189,523	372,192	368,726	1,063,209
1952	309,181	185,748	219,853	428,713	384,434	1,154,129
1953	361,465	218,376	248,309	492,856	392,576	1,340,149
1954	416,707	248,458	278,068	563,975	408,327	1,589,424
1955	492,638	282,671	309,785	643,631	434,871	1,804,413
1956	559,182	311,828	339,700	718,090	458,953	2,012,227
1957	648,799	347,410	372,579	808,651	474,294	2,288,507

TABLE B.6 CONSUMERS' STOCKS BY STATES: WASHING MACHINES, 1944–57
(continued)

Year	Montana	Idaho	Wyoming	Colorado	New Mexico	Arizona
1944	79,474	67,380	29,371	164,132	27,643	63,925
1945	79,198	67,146	29,269	163,561	27,548	63,703
1946	85,970	71,623	31,428	179,090	30,922	69,243
1947	94,652	78,453	34,530	197,278	36,455	77,689
1948	105,813	88,417	38,640	235,599	41,998	89,933
1949	112,779	96,564	41,557	251,879	47,734	98,786
1950	121,497	106,260	45,431	275,613	56,698	112,110
1951	126,191	111,546	48,669	293,937	65,503	123,063
1952	132,289	118,616	51,712	310,340	75,117	137,981
1953	137,098	122,504	53,672	328,707	86,678	153,887
1954	143,617	128,667	55,828	351,582	99,450	178,589
1955	151,473	136,710	57,706	378,648	118,266	193,646
1956	154,636	142,188	60,775	403,996	134,682	211,814
1957	159,274	150,308	63,387	435,879	151,616	238,581

Year	Utah	Nevada	Washington	Oregon	California
1944	126,122	13,822	333,447	183,136	1,297,506
1945	125,684	13,774	332,288	182,498	1,292,996
1946	134,936	15,765	360,609	200,329	1,411,426
1947	146,754	18,228	399,219	223,219	1,599,845
1948	165,222	21,142	447,067	269,901	1,836,888
1949	175,512	24,889	480,614	291,896	1,987,196
1950	189,557	29,493	523,964	322,171	2,202,037
1951	195,323	34,452	555,767	345,521	2,404,799
1952	204,321	39,650	588,736	374,160	2,643,378
1953	207,536	45,664	619,372	399,978	2,882,134
1954	212,552	53,960	669,914	423,535	3,118,232
1955	221,362	61,750	717,430	445,519	3,334,115
1956	226,565	67,114	738,723	473,392	3,621,883
1957	227,983	74,006	772,601	504,712	3,980,598

TABLE B.7 Consumers' Stocks by States: Electric Water Heaters, 1945–57

Year	Maine	New Hampshire	Vermont	Massachusetts	Rhode Island	Connecticut
1945	10,767	8,587	5,274	27,554	4,108	19,515
1946	11,863	8,209	5,326	28,942	5,832	21,207
1947	18,354	11,533	8,593	37,418	8,013	36,308
1948	28,507	13,756	10,972	46,066	10,720	51,368
1949	32,539	18,323	11,847	60,916	13,074	60,806
1950	37,626	20,929	12,621	83,210	15,901	72,871
1951	42,431	22,929	14,347	97,062	18,718	84,397
1952	43,375	23,046	13,713	113,505	20,085	93,023
1953	46,871	25,292	14,519	127,529	21,463	101,995
1954	49,706	26,371	14,704	136,290	22,176	106,565
1955	55,014	28,806	16,177	151,551	24,265	116,035
1956	59,969	31,114	18,060	162,296	26,398	122,312
1957	61,283	31,565	20,797	167,393	27,153	124,954

Year	New York	New Jersey	Pennsylvania	Ohio	Indiana	Illinois
1945	49,114	14,141	82,563	90,914	47,652	65,729
1946	53,383	16,587	87,588	100,497	48,581	70,380
1947	93,106	39,065	166,289	168,638	103,595	128,498
1948	129,200	54,837	234,414	210,373	142,020	164,530
1949	157,246	66,425	281,820	236,757	166,281	189,365
1950	189,859	83,157	346,833	277,862	200,999	215,678
1951	224,503	97,957	400,594	313,972	237,611	237,833
1952	256,441	112,084	453,054	349,412	254,154	257,923
1953	286,542	123,147	499,288	384,525	282,125	277,973
1954	306,703	129,377	530,914	400,729	301,914	283,134
1955	340,209	140,039	576,151	439,012	333,693	294,787
1956	364,094	146,698	607,044	461,363	351,729	296,649
1957	374,171	154,857	620,100	482,398	365,586	298,239

TABLE B.7 CONSUMERS' STOCKS BY STATES: ELECTRIC WATER HEATERS,
1945–57   *(continued)*

Year	Michigan	Wisconsin	Minnesota	Iowa	Missouri	North Dakota
1945	106,377	46,329	40,035	17,822	28,936	6,280
1946	110,786	43,761	41,027	21,899	39,541	6,282
1947	153,908	82,822	82,382	56,444	68,791	10,539
1948	182,385	116,343	111,696	86,357	94,246	17,837
1949	200,173	141,147	125,681	108,610	110,641	21,943
1950	218,422	171,659	142,487	135,335	130,539	26,510
1951	239,534	196,404	154,200	157,505	152,326	31,732
1952	239,760	214,182	163,097	176,484	171,696	36,202
1953	263,248	237,527	175,606	193,757	184,958	40,291
1954	269,561	254,460	182,621	204,492	190,830	44,597
1955	296,934	275,199	191,718	216,154	201,175	49,828
1956	316,931	289,413	199,668	219,745	205,874	53,669
1957	335,018	297,368	205,058	221,071	205,363	55,824

Year	South Dakota	Nebraska	Kansas	Delaware, Maryland and District of Columbia	Virginia	West Virginia
1945	6,536	4,485	8,990	5,933	21,302	7,232
1946	6,344	7,520	10,212	15,511	23,873	10,617
1947	12,792	23,527	18,752	38,203	49,806	22,353
1948	19,882	37,188	24,795	54,550	75,965	35,128
1949	25,908	46,024	28,123	66,199	96,518	42,134
1950	32,956	57,822	31,127	84,976	121,829	53,320
1951	39,522	66,607	34,584	103,099	140,140	63,711
1952	46,285	74,308	37,114	120,867	165,197	73,346
1953	51,803	80,231	38,075	133,552	186,994	81,016
1954	56,642	83,229	36,736	141,987	203,462	84,069
1955	61,862	86,921	37,311	159,995	232,478	94,165
1956	65,462	88,116	36,597	172,163	257,130	105,424
1957	67,536	86,762	37,074	169,120	283,399	116,963

TABLE B.7 Consumers' Stocks by States: Electric Water Heaters, 1945–57 *(continued)*

Year	North Carolina and South Carolina	Georgia	Florida	Kentucky	Tennessee	Alabama
1945	44,890	25,900	33,156	5,332	34,726	18,077
1946	48,163	27,418	34,234	8,176	38,283	18,569
1947	102,073	59,770	79,248	19,867	78,002	41,025
1948	170,241	89,400	121,942	32,578	111,001	60,104
1949	224,163	107,188	149,326	40,659	130,984	72,715
1950	298,919	135,276	196,257	53,510	145,465	90,114
1951	363,772	164,232	244,421	62,984	168,443	104,430
1952	429,753	192,815	288,783	75,208	200,654	118,275
1953	495,087	213,547	334,729	85,732	217,279	129,095
1954	558,093	228,972	382,356	91,779	224,430	136,263
1955	669,371	248,513	443,738	100,650	242,454	149,025
1956	770,489	262,861	497,667	109,196	261,757	158,905
1957	899,763	278,902	538,317	121,494	274,180	166,620

Year	Mississippi	Arkansas	Louisiana	Oklahoma	Texas	Montana
1945	3,879	1,831	1,117	1,434	13,509	7,434
1946	5,533	3,496	2,995	2,940	20,860	7,976
1947	10,857	8,805	5,124	4,929	35,873	13,315
1948	17,436	13,643	7,640	7,962	50,736	18,005
1949	20,511	17,478	9,871	10,088	59,541	21,058
1950	24,449	21,372	12,078	11,638	71,216	23,865
1951	27,572	24,362	14,257	12,754	81,405	25,184
1952	30,776	26,687	15,870	13,865	89,745	26,747
1953	32,895	27,920	17,019	14,118	94,970	29,044
1954	32,844	27,817	17,734	13,512	98,310	29,688
1955	34,657	28,319	19,648	14,202	109,178	33,076
1956	37,062	28,689	21,611	15,147	117,235	35,226
1957	39,651	29,260	24,547	16,175	128,939	37,206

TABLE B.7 Consumers' Stocks by States: Electric Water Heaters, 1945–57 *(continued)*

Year	Idaho	Wyoming	Colorado	New Mexico	Arizona	Utah
1945	12,476	1,239	5,250	648	1,823	12,847
1946	13,409	1,954	7,353	1,074	2,495	14,448
1947	27,586	2,754	20,267	2,148	7,905	29,642
1948	39,920	4,126	29,743	3,398	14,811	40,145
1949	47,733	4,889	37,030	4,560	16,536	47,115
1950	54,972	5,489	45,816	5,915	18,163	56,305
1951	58,860	6,052	52,288	7,326	19,474	61,633
1952	60,310	6,584	58,154	8,600	17,464	67,477
1953	64,138	6,885	61,878	9,665	18,618	73,027
1954	66,990	6,660	63,490	10,286	18,849	74,458
1955	73,053	7,006	66,059	11,682	19,526	77,805
1956	75,846	7,351	66,303	13,044	19,726	78,062
1957	82,945	8,017	67,446	16,023	20,533	81,604

Year	Nevada	Washington	Oregon	California
1945	2,452	56,490	33,730	35,594
1946	2,867	58,491	37,720	44,486
1947	8,234	98,371	65,639	108,896
1948	11,045	129,910	97,934	136,125
1949	13,626	149,667	115,728	152,011
1950	16,159	166,777	134,288	172,473
1951	21,710	176,170	146,790	195,076
1952	26,969	186,665	158,960	212,656
1953	31,508	203,297	167,375	226,678
1954	35,354	223,376	170,214	232,230
1955	39,442	258,456	188,812	245,949
1956	42,101	283,186	201,352	254,286
1957	43,906	301,488	208,561	255,478

BIBLIOGRAPHY

A. General

ADDISON, W. *See* Nerlove.

BORING, E.G. "Gustav Theodor Fechner," reprinted in J. R. Newman, ed., *The World of Mathematics*, New York: Simon and Schuster, 1956, Vol. 2.

BRUMBERG, R. *See* Modigliani.

CHOW, G. *Demand for Automobiles in the United States*, Amsterdam: North-Holland Publishing Co., 1957.

COCHRANE, D. AND G. H. ORCUTT. "Applications of Least-Squares Regression to Relationships Containing Auto-Correlated Error Terms," *Journal of the American Statistical Association*, 44 (March, 1949), No. 245.

FISHER, F. M. *A Priori Information and Time Series Analysis*, Amsterdam: North-Holland Publishing Co., 1962.

———. "On the Cost of Approximate Specification in Simultaneous Equation Estimation," *Econometrica*, 29 (1961).

FRIEDMAN, M. *A Theory of the Consumption Function*, Princeton: Princeton University Press (for National Bureau for Economic Research), 1957.

GRILICHES, Z. "The Demand for a Durable Input: Farm Tractors in the United States, 1921–57," in A. C. Harberger, ed., *The Demand for Durable Goods*, Chicago: University of Chicago Press, 1960.

HOUTHAKKER, H. S. "Some Calculations on Electricity Consumption in Great Britain," *Journal of the Royal Statistical Society*, Series A (General), CXIV (1951), Part 3.

KUH, E. "Some Notes on Cross-Sections, Time Series and the Specification of Variables," paper presented before the Cleveland meetings of the Econometric Society, December, 1956.

———. "The Validity of Cross-Sectionally Estimated Behavior Equations in Time Series Applications," *Econometrica*, 27 (April, 1959), No. 2.

LIPPITT, V. *Determinants of Consumer Demand for House Furnishings and Equipment*. Cambridge: Harvard University Press, 1959.

MODIGLIANI, F. AND R. BRUMBERG. "Utility Analysis and the Consumption Function: An Interpretation of Cross-Section Data," in K. Kurihara, ed., *Post-Keynesian Economics*, New Brunswick: Rutgers University Press, 1954.

NERLOVE, M. AND W. ADDISON. "Statistical Estimation of Long-Run Elasticities of Supply and Demand," *Journal of Farm Economics*, XL (November, 1958), No. 4.

ORCUTT, G. H. *See* Cochrane.

ROWE, D. A. *See* Stone.

STONE, J. R. N. AND D. A. ROWE. "The Market Demand for Durable Goods," *Econometrica*, 25 (July, 1957), No. 3.

WORKING, E. J. *The Demand for Meat*. Chicago: Institute of Meat Packing, 1954.

B. Data Sources

AMERICAN GAS ASSOCIATION. *Gas Facts.*

AMERICAN GAS ASSOCIATION, BUREAU OF STATISTICS. *Historical Statistics of the Gas Industry.* New York: 1956.

COMMONWEALTH OF MASSACHUSETTS, OFFICE OF THE SECRETARY. *Annual Report on the Vital Statistics of Massachusetts.*

EDISON ELECTRIC INSTITUTE. *Statistical Bulletin.*

GENERAL ELECTRIC COMPANY. *General Electric Diary.*

GRAHAM, R. E., Jr. *See* Schwartz.

———. "Regional Income Distribution in 1957," *Survey of Current Business, 38* (August, 1958), No. 8.

MCGRAW-HILL PUBLISHING COMPANY. *Electrical Merchandising.*

SCHWARTZ, C. F. AND R.E. GRAHAM, Jr. *Personal Income by States since 1929,* a supplement to the *Survey of Current Business,* 1956.

UNITED STATES GOVERNMENT, BOARD OF GOVERNORS OF THE FEDERAL RESERVE SYSTEM. *Federal Reserve Bulletin.*

UNITED STATES GOVERNMENT, DEPARTMENT OF COMMERCE, BUREAU OF THE CENSUS. *Annual Survey of Manufactures.*

———. *Census of Manufactures.*

———. *Census of Mineral Industries.*

———. *Statistical Abstract of the United States.*

UNITED STATES GOVERNMENT, FEDERAL POWER COMMISSION. *Statistics of Electric Utilities in the United States.*

INDEX

Addison, W., 74
Aggregation of demand over
   commodities, 122
   establishments, 121, 123–125
   households, 153
   individuals, 153
   products, 121–123
   white goods, 153
American Gas Association, 88
Annual Survey of Manufactures, 130, 143
Appliances
   (*see :* White good, types of)

Beaton, A. E., Jr., ix
Bolker, J. L., ix
Boring, E. G., 16
Brumberg, R., 75
Bureau of Labor Statistics, Wholesale Price Index, 86–87

Census of Manufactures, 143
Census of als Mineral Industries, 134
Chow, G., 76
Cochrane, D., 23
Commerce Department, 29
Composition of industrial output, 121–122, 127–128
   geographic adjustments in, 129
Constant technology model of industrial electricity demand, 120–141
   aggregation problems, 120–125
   estimating procedures, 125–134
   results, 134–142
Cook, L., vii
Covariance analysis, 1, 3, 36, 38, 48, 89
Cross-section data, 126–131, 134
   estimates, 133
   moving, 129–130

Demographic variables, 5, 96, 112
   marriages, 8, 96, 103, 112
   population, 113

wired households, 5, 75, 77, 113–114, 116–117
Disease model, 80–85, 91
   quality change in, 84–85
   rate of growth of, 80
   (*see :* White goods "disease")
Dishwashers
   (*see :* White goods, types of)
Dryers
   (*see :* White goods, types of)

Eberhard, W. C., ix
Economic variables, 5, 8, 96, 100
Economically older *vs.* economically younger states in household electricity demand, 52, 57–58
Edison Electric Institute, 28, 52, 87–88, 130
Electric appliances
   (*see :* White goods, types of)
Electrical Merchandising, 61–62, 66, 68–72, 86, 92
Electricity customers, number of, 78
Electricity demand
   data and results, 28–52, 91–113
   elasticity of, 136–137
   growth rates in, 8, 33, 41, 57, 90–92, 119
   by households, 2–5, 8–9, 10–60, 117–119
      long-run, 4–5, 73–119
      short-run, 2–4, 10–60, 117–118
   by industry, 6–9, 119–149
      constant technology, 6–7, 120–142
      technological change, 7–8, 142–149
Electricity generated by industry
   (*see :* self-generated electricity)
Electricity inputs, 6–9, 120–123, 125, 131, 143–149
Electricity-intensive goods, 139–140, 144–145
Electrification, rate of, 113–117
   regressions for, 115–116

End-of-year stocks, 62–64, 69–71
Estimating procedures for
    household long-run electricity
    demand, 4–7, 73–119
    household short-run electricity
    demand, 2–4, 10–60
    industry electricity demand, 120-
    149
Extractive industries, 141–142

Federal Power Commission, 28, 43,
    130
Federal Reserve Index of Manufac-
    turing Production, 145
First differences, 2, 23–27, 29, 41, 79
Fisher, F. M., vii, 24, 26, 41, 126
Freezers
    (see : White goods, types of)
Friedman, M., 15, 75–76, 86
Frying pans
    (see : White goods, types of)

Gas-using appliances, 75–76, 78–79,
    87, 100, 103, 109–110
    ranges, 103
    refrigerators, 100, 110
General Electric Corporation Re-
    search Laboratory, vii
Graham, R. E., Jr., 29
Griliches, Z., ix, 46, 79
Growth rates of demand for white
    goods, 33, 41, 57, 119

Harberger, A. C., 29
Harvard University Littauer Statis-
    tical Laboratory, ix
Hofmeister, R., ix
Homogeneity, 39–41, 48–49, 89–92,
    109, 128, 130, 142
    hypothesis, 38
    inhomogeneity, 48–50, 90–91, 96
    109, 128
    lack of, 38–39
    test for, 28, 38–42, 48–50
Household electricity demand, 10–
    60, 73–119
    long-run, 4–5, 73–119
    short-run, 2–4, 10–60

    short-run regressions, 42, 50,
    53–55
    long-run regressions, 101–108
    variables, 5, 95
Households, average age of, 75
    number of, 8, 75
Houthakker, H. S., 24

Income, current, 5, 112, 117
    long-run, 5, 112, 117
    permanent, 81
Income elasticities of household
    short-run electricity demand,
    37, 42–43, 48, 50, 57–58
    negative, 42–43, 48, 50
    rural vs. urban, 43, 50, 57
Income threshold, 81, 100, 112, 117
Income variables, 75, 112
Industry regressions, 135
    extractive industries, 141
    two-digit industries, 135
Ironers
    (see : White goods, types of)
Iterative estimation techniques,
    125–126, 130

Kendall, M. G., 38
Kingdon, K., vii
Kinnell, A. L., ix
Korean War, effect of, on stocks of
    appliances, 63, 65, 88–89
Kuh, E., 38, 128
Kurihara, K., 75

Lighting fixtures
    (see : White goods, types of)
Lippitt, V., 61
Locational decisions, 126–127, 131,
    134

McGraw-Hill Book Company, Inc.
    (see : Electrical Merchandising)
Marriages, number of, 5, 8, 78, 83, 87
Modigliani, F., 75
Mood, A. M., 38
Multicollinearity, 3, 23, 126

National Bureau for Economic Re-
    search, 15

Nerlove, M., 74
Newman, J. R., 16

Operating costs of appliances, 110–111
Orcutt, G. H., 23

Population, changes in, 5, 113
Price of appliances, 5
Price elasticity
    of household electricity demand, 58, 96, 100, 109, 113, 117–119
    economically older *vs.* economically younger states, 52, 57–58
    rural *vs.* urban states, 3–4, 43–48, 50–51, 59, 96
    of industrial electricity demand, 120–149
Price and rate schedules for electricity, 5–9, 12, 24–25, 56, 59, 73, 75, 96, 100, 109, 113, 118, 121–123, 128, 131, 138, 140–144, 146–148
Price of gas, 75
    coefficient of, 109
Primary metal industries, 130–131

Quality change, 84–85

Radios
    (*see :* White goods, types of)
Ranges
    (*see :* White goods, types of)
Refrigerators, 62–66
    (*see:* White goods, types of)
    end-of-year stock, 62–64
    and Korean War, 63, 65
    oldest existing, 65
    sales, 62–63
    scrapping age, 63–66
Regression technique, 3
Rowe, D. A., 74, 78–79
Rural states, 3–4, 43–48, 50, 96
Rural-urban differences in household short-run demand for electricity, 44–47, 51, 59

Schwartz, C. F., 29

Scott, B., ix
Scrapping age,
    freezers, 69
    ranges, 70
    refrigerators, 63–66
    washers, 64
    water heaters, 69–70
Self-generated electricity, 122–123, 130, 143, 146
Statistical Abstract of the United States, 114
Stock adjustment model, 73–75, 79–80
Stone, J. R. N., 74, 78–79

Technological change, 6–8, 120, 126, 133, 142–149
    measure of, 143
Technology, constant, 6, 120–125, 147
Television sets
    (*see :* White goods, types of)
Tennessee Valley Authority, 100, 118–119
Three-digit industry, 122, 134, 143
Threshold income
    (*see :* income threshold)
Travis, C., ix
Two-digit industry, 6–7, 130–147

Urban population, 35–36, 48
Urban states, 3–4, 44–47, 50, 96
Urbanization, degree of, 3–4, 35–37, 42–45, 48, 50

Washers
    (*see :* White goods, types of)
Water heaters
    (*see :* White goods, types of)
Weber-Fechner hypothesis, 16, 51
White goods, definition of, 10
    demographic variables in demand for, 5, 8, 75, 77, 96, 103, 112–114, 116–117
    "disease" model, 80, 83–85, 91, 103
    economic variables in demand for, 5, 8, 96, 100

estimate of demand curves for, 2, 23
substitutes for (*see*: Gas-using appliances)
White goods services, demand for, 10–60, 73, 78, 80
power requirements of, 76
price of, 75–76
sales of, 92
substitutes for, 12
White goods stock, 17, 21–23, 25–26, 33–34, 43–47, 61, 71, 73, 78, 80, 90, 92, 103, 113, 118, 153
effect of income on, 44–48
rural composition of, 3–4, 44–47
rural *vs*. urban, 44–47, 51
urban composition of, 3–4, 44–47
White goods, types of
dishwashers, 11
dryers, 4, 12, 61, 67–69, 86–87, 109–110, 154–157
freezers, 2, 4, 11–12, 44–45, 61, 68–69, 109, 158–161
frying pans, 43

ironers, 4, 61, 67, 72, 86, 100–103, 111–112, 162–165
lighting fixtures, 22, 43, 45, 59
radios, 61
ranges, 2, 4–5, 12, 61, 66–67, 70, 72, 87, 100, 103–104, 108–111, 166–169
refrigerators, 4–5, 10–11, 13, 22, 43, 45, 61–66, 71, 84–85, 87, 96–100, 109–111, 170–173
television sets, 11, 43–45, 61
vacuum cleaners, 59
washers, 2, 4, 44, 59, 61, 64, 66, 71–72, 84, 86, 88, 93–96, 100–111, 174–177
water heaters, 4–5, 61, 69–70, 72, 86–88, 109–110, 178–181
Willson, C. H., ix
Wired households
changes in, 5
cost of wiring, 114, 116
number of, 75, 77, 113–114, 116–117
(*see*: Electrification, rate of)
Working, E. J., 15